A Milliner Learning Straw Sewing

RUSSELL SAGE
FOUNDATION

WORKING GIRLS IN EVENING SCHOOLS

A STATISTICAL STUDY

BY

MARY VAN KLEECK

SECRETARY COMMITTEE ON WOMEN'S WORK
RUSSELL SAGE FOUNDATION

NEW YORK
SURVEY ASSOCIATES, INC.
MCMXIV

THE TROW PRESS
NEW YORK

TABLE OF CONTENTS

APPENDICES

LIST OF ILLUSTRATIONS

Photographs by Lewis W. Hine

LIST OF TABLES

LIST OF TABLES

LIST OF TABLES

APPENDIX I

LIST OF TABLES

LIST OF TABLES

INTRODUCTION

IN the hope of supplying facts to clarify public thinking and to point the way toward the solution of certain industrial problems, the Russell Sage Foundation has undertaken to make a series of type-studies of the occupations of women in New York. The results of two of these studies have already been published under the titles Women in the Bookbinding Trade, and Artificial Flower Makers.* These volumes represent detailed inquiries into the conditions of women's work in two distinct trades.

The present study, that of Working Girls in Public Evening Schools, is of a different character. It is not an intensive investigation of girls in any one occupation, but an extensive view of the workers in the many fields of employment represented among the women who attend evening school. As a study of wage-earning women who are seeking to supplement an inadequate education, the facts secured relate especially to the problems of industrial training.

Every year from autumn until spring more than a hundred public school buildings in New York

* Van Kleeck, Mary: Women in the Bookbinding Trade. Artificial Flower Makers. Russell Sage Foundation Publications. New York, Survey Associates, 1913.

are open four nights a week to pupils of various ages, from fourteen to seventy or older, who can not attend day school. In the year 1910–11, when this investigation was made, 33 of these public night schools were organized for women only, and 42 others admitted both men and women.* Nearly 50,000 women, chiefly wage-earners, were enrolled in the classes, some of whom stayed only one night, while some continued more or less regularly throughout the term.† Owing to irregular attendance and varying dates of entrance, the number present on any one night is much smaller than the enrollment for the year. Nevertheless, in no other public institution in New York, as far as we know, would it be possible to reach simultaneously so large a group of wage-earning women as are to be found in these class rooms.

We believed that a record of the occupations of a fair proportion of these women and the correlation of the data secured with facts about their ages, nationality, hours of labor, and previous schooling, would afford a foundation for further intensive study. We believed, furthermore, that such an investigation would be useful in demonstrating the possible value of the evening schools as experiment stations in education. Similar types of pupils and the same groups of occupations would

* Superintendent of Schools, New York City. Thirteenth Annual Report, 1910–11. Report on Evening Schools for the Year Ending July 31, 1911, pp. 5–6.

† Ibid. Compiled from Table I, pp. 20–24. Detailed statement, Enrollment of Women and Girls.

probably be represented in the day continuation schools, whose development is now being advocated as part of a system of industrial training. At present, few seem to realize how much the public evening schools have to offer in experience and facts as a basis for planning new types of industrial courses.

The method of investigation was to distribute card records containing questions to be answered in writing by women in each class room in the schools selected.* This was done in the autumn of 1910, under the direction of the teachers, after members of our staff had visited each school and fully explained the plan to the principal. The questions asked are shown on the record card which is reproduced in the appendix.† They included such personal items as age, country of birth, and number of years in the United States, detailed information about schools attended, and a carefully planned set of questions designed to reveal that elusive fact—the actual occupation of a worker in our complex industrial system.

For several reasons, no questions were asked about wages. We feared that if we asked how much they earned the girls might raise objections which would jeopardize the whole inquiry, since the wage received is considered by many to be a strictly personal matter. Moreover, it seemed doubtful whether data on this point would be

* See p. 6, for statement of number of schools included.

† For facsimile of card record see Appendix, p. 186.

accurate, unless the filling of the records could be supervised by an investigator familiar with all the intricacies of wage statistics.

The questions on the cards were answered by 13,737 girls. Some preliminary experimenting had been necessary to make a schedule which would yield reliable information. Realizing the difficulties involved in the method of investigation pursued,—the risk of misinterpretation or misunderstanding on the part of the many thousands who in the class rooms of nearly 50 different school buildings would be called upon to write their answers,—we determined to test the questions thoroughly before having the cards printed. Through the co-operation of several leaders of girls' clubs in social settlements, typewritten schedules were distributed at club meetings. More than a hundred were returned, and through an analysis of the answers a card record was gradually evolved so simple in form that in spite of the brief schooling of many of the pupils who answered the questions 13,141 of the 13,737 records secured were accurate and complete enough for tabulation. They were carefully read to discover discrepancies or errors, and were classified first by schools, and then by large occupational groups.

For reasons already suggested, it is not easy to determine just how large a proportion this group of 13,000 women forms of the total number in attendance during the year in the schools included in the investigation. The annual report of the city superintendent of schools for that year states for each evening school the enrollment, the register, and the average attendance. Every prospective student who records her application for entrance into an evening class is counted among the number "enrolled." The enrollment of women in 1910–11, as previously noted, was nearly 50,000. Some of these never appeared in a class room. The word "register" is used for the number who actually attend any length of time, whether their stay be one night or five months. The "average attendance" is computed by adding together the number of pupils actually present each evening throughout the school year, and dividing by the number of evenings the schools are open. None of these figures shows the actual attendance at any given date.*

Furthermore, although in our investigation we made an effort at first to have all the records filled on the same day, conditions in the different schools made it impossible to carry out this plan. The dates on the record cards show that although all were filled during the autumn, the work was done on different evenings in September, October, and November. In some instances blank records were kept in the principal's office to be filled from time to time by girls who entered later in the term. Because of these variations and because of the

* For further discussion of average register and attendance, see pp. 142 ff.

well-known irregularity of attendance in evening classes, a comparison of the number of records secured with the figures given in the annual report of the superintendent of schools for "average attendance" or "register," throws more light on evening school problems than on the scope of this investigation. Nevertheless, Table 1 is presented to show the number of women registered, the average attendance, and the number who filled records in the schools included in the inquiry.

Thus, the total register of women in the schools included in the investigation in the winter of 1910–11 was 39,242, while the average attendance was 15,665. The number of women filling record cards used in the tabulation was 13,141, 33 per cent of the total register, but 84 per cent of the average attendance. With the exception of the Long Island City Trade School, the only one investigated in the borough of Queens, the inquiry was confined to the three boroughs of Manhattan, the Bronx, and Brooklyn, and covered all evening schools in these boroughs except two elementary schools in very remote sections of Brooklyn and three located far uptown in the Bronx. The conditions in these latter districts, as in Queens and Richmond, differ markedly from those of the more congested sections of the city.*

In the spring of 1911 our investigators returned to most of the schools in Manhattan to secure

* For list of schools investigated, register, average attendance, and number of record cards secured in each school, see Appendix I, Table B, p. 190.

TABLE 1.—PUBLIC EVENING SCHOOLS INCLUDED IN THE INVESTIGATION, REGISTRATION, AND AVERAGE ATTENDANCE OF WOMEN IN THESE SCHOOLS DURING THE REGULAR TERM, AND NUMBER OF WOMEN FOR WHOM RECORDS WERE TABULATED, BY LOCATION AND TYPE OF SCHOOL[a]

Location and type of school	SCHOOLS INCLUDED IN THE INVESTIGATION			Women for whom records were tabulated
	Number	Register of women	Average attendance of women	
Manhattan and the Bronx:				
High and trade schools .	4	5,776[b]	2,330	2,587
Elementary schools. .	21	19,388	7,733	5,059
Total	25	25,164	10,063	7,646
Brooklyn and Long Island City:				
High and trade schools .	5	4,134[c]	1,599	2,275
Elementary schools. .	18	9,944	4,003	3,220
Total	23	14,078	5,602	5,495
All schools:				
High and trade schools .	9	9,910	3,929	4,862
Elementary schools. .	39	29,332	11,736	8,279
Total	48	39,242	15,665	13,141

[a] Data appear in detail in Appendix I, Table B, p. 190.

[b] In one mixed high school the registration of women was not stated separately from that of men. The number of women enrolled has been substituted, as there is usually no material difference between the two sets of figures.

[c] The number of women registered was not available for two mixed trade schools. In one case, the number of women enrolled was used in place of the number registered, and in the other, the number of women registered was estimated by assuming that this number bore the same relation to the total register that the average attendance of women bore to the total average attendance.

records of the length of attendance of each girl who had filled out a card in the preceding autumn. This part of the work was time-consuming, as in the majority of schools it was necessary to copy the facts about each girl from teachers' roll books, which offered the material in less convenient form than does the card system since introduced.*

To verify the data on the card records, a group of 260 of the girls included in the study were interviewed at their homes during the spring and summer of 1911. The total number of visits to homes was 331. In connection with other industrial studies made by the same investigators many more of these girls have been visited, some of them during the spring of 1913. The results of these interviews have been most satisfactory in corroborating the information given in writing on the original cards.†

The investigation in the schools was made possible through the courteous co-operation of Dr. John H. Haaren, associate city superintendent in charge of evening schools, to whom our thanks are due. To the principals and teachers we are greatly indebted for the time given to supervising pupils who answered the questions. We wish to express

* The total number of visits made to the schools, at this time and in the preceding autumn, was 178. As a matter of fact, this figure is an understatement, since in securing records of attendance three or four members of the staff went together in order to facilitate the clerical work. Counting each person's visit as one, the total number was 247.

† The facts about the evening classes in the Manhattan Trade School for Girls, discussed in Chapter V, were secured in the spring of 1913 at the beginning of an interesting experiment in that school.

appreciation also to Dr. Albert Shiels who became district superintendent in charge of evening schools the year following our investigation, and who, from time to time, has supplied us with information needed in the preparation of these chapters.

The members of the staff who took part in the field work were Miss Louise C. Odencrantz, Miss Alice P. Barrows, and Miss Elizabeth L. Meigs. The statistical work, which is so important a part of this book, was done under the direction of Miss Odencrantz.

In reading the chapters which follow, it should be remembered that the subject of investigation was not the evening schools and their methods, but the occupations of the girls and women attending them. We desire to be judged not as school investigators, but as students of the industrial problems represented in a particular group of wage-earning girls who were enrolled for one year in evening classes of the New York public school system.

CHAPTER I

EVENING SCHOOLS AND THE GIRLS WHO ATTEND THEM

THE gay throngs of children who march merrily out from the school buildings in the afternoon afford no more inspiring sight than the more restrained and sober groups of older pupils who enter the same class rooms in the evening. Natives of Russia, Croatia, Italy, or Turkey who are eager to learn English; youngsters who have left day school before completing even the elementary grades; grown men and women who never went to school in their childhood; ambitious students preparing for examinations for civil service appointments, for state regents' diplomas, or for admission to colleges or technical schools; boys who want practice in carpentry or metal work, and girls who wish to make their own hats or dresses,—all come with their varied needs and aspirations in search of more education.* Some of them are desperately in earnest, eager for every crumb of knowledge, making tremendous sacrifices of strength to come every night from

* Attendance in public evening schools in New York is voluntary for all except boys under sixteen who have left school before graduating from the grammar grades; for them attendance is compulsory. See also footnote, p. 74.

Monday to Thursday and every week from autumn until spring,* however exhausted they may be after the day's work in shop or factory. Among others ambition shows less persistence and the good resolution which led them to register perishes prematurely. Some have wandered into the school building without any very serious purpose or definite aim in view, and unless the teacher can arouse their interest, they join the ranks of the irregular attendants, who are the despair of the school authorities. Nevertheless, whether they be eager or indifferent, serious or frivolous, studious or lazy in their school work, they are representative of the wage-earners of the community, and, as such, their ambitions and their hopes present to educators a variety of problems as absorbing in interest as they are vital in importance.

The method of teaching English composition to a child in the seventh grade has been more carefully studied and standardized than has that of giving belated instruction in spelling and writing to a woman whose experience in life has already taught her many things beyond the ken of school children. Consider, for example, the married woman enrolled in an English class, who, besides serving as cook and housekeeper, is enabled by her skill in gold-leaf laying to support herself and her

* In evening elementary schools the term begins the first Monday in October and continues for 90 evenings until March or early April, according to the place of Easter on the calendar. In evening high schools and trade schools the session lasts 120 evenings, from the third Monday in September until May. Summer classes in English for foreigners are a recent innovation.

sick husband. Instruction in the English language offered an Italian girl who began work packing olives the day after she landed in New York, involves more than a lesson in words, phrases, and grammatical construction. It should include an interpretation of the ways and thoughts of a new land to a pupil who has had no opportunity to find out how much of the United States lies outside of Canal Street. When the class confronting the English teacher includes not only Italian olive packers, but Hungarian vest makers, Bohemian cigar makers, and Russian milliners and shirtwaist makers, the task of giving them a common voice and a common understanding of their new environment demands the insight of a prophet.

Or again, the young American girl whose ways of thinking were more or less clear to the seventh grade teacher in day school last year has acquired a different point of view now that she has become a wage-earner. Instinctively she demands that the change which new experiences have wrought in her shall be recognized when she joins a class in evening school. But perhaps most difficult of all the problems encountered by teachers in evening schools is the restless and undirected seeking after some kind of training that shall enable the wage-earner to find a better job, or to get ahead in the one he or she now has. Thus, not only previous schooling, but age, nationality, and occupation, are important factors in determining the needs of evening school pupils.

ENTRANCE REQUIREMENTS AND COURSES OFFERED

It is on the basis of the amount of the pupils' previous education that the regular evening schools at present are distinguished as "elementary" or "high." In addition, there are the evening "trade" schools, this term applying to schools of elementary grade in which trade courses are offered. For admission to an evening high school it is necessary to be a graduate of an elementary school or to have an equivalent preparation. In evening elementary schools no preparation other than the wish to attend is required, and the diversity of mental equipment of the pupils is, therefore, wide.* An effort is made, however, in forming classes, to group together those whose previous training is somewhat similar, especially in the case of boys or girls under sixteen who left day school before graduating. They are enrolled in the classes for instruction in what are known as "common branches." For boys under sixteen who have not finished the elementary grades, the law, as we have seen, requires this kind of instruction.

In general, the courses offered vary according to the demands of the pupils in the different schools. The evening high school curriculum includes such academic subjects as languages and science; commercial courses, like stenography, typewriting, bookkeeping, and commercial law;

* The schooling of the girls investigated will be discussed in Chapter IV.

and, for women, courses in domestic arts and sciences.

In the evening trade schools a greater variety of courses is offered to men than to women. A young man may have an opportunity to enter a class in blacksmithing, cabinet making, carpentry and joinery, electric engineering, electrical installation, gas engine construction, pattern making, plumbing, printing, or steam engineering. For women, the opportunities in trade training are chiefly limited to millinery, dressmaking, and costume designing, although there is manifest a growing desire on the part of school authorities to extend the industrial courses for women to other occupations.*

In the evening elementary schools the subjects taught include English to foreigners, the "common branches," and special subjects similar to those taught in the high schools but planned for students whose previous training would not be sufficient for admission to high school. These courses include shop work, cooking, dressmaking, millinery, drawing, stenography, typewriting, and bookkeeping. Some of these, as, for example, stenography, have been introduced into certain elementary schools, not because they can be taught satisfactorily to

* In the autumn of 1913, the New York Evening School of Industrial Art was opened to give "courses for men and women engaged in occupations involving the adaptation of art to industries." (Board of Education, New York. Report of the President, January, 1914, p. 21.) The courses offered included decoration, drawing, book illustration, and designing of costumes, jewelry, stained glass, textiles, wall paper, wood work, and plastic work.

Learning to Make Their Own Hats

A Class in Home Dressmaking

pupils who have never completed the elementary grades, but because no evening high school is open in the neighborhood to meet the demand from pupils who have the necessary preparation.

The high schools were far apart, and many who would have been eligible for attendance in them were obliged to be content with the nearest elementary school, or to forego instruction in the evening.* In 1910–11 the Bronx had one evening high school open to men and women, Queens one, and Staten Island one. In Brooklyn there were three for women only and one mixed school to which women were admitted. Three for women only were in Manhattan, one at 114th Street and Seventh Avenue, one in Forty-first Street near Third Avenue, and one on the lower East Side, on the corner of Hester and Essex streets. The evening elementary schools were much more numerous.

NATIONALITIES IN THE SCHOOLS

The location of the evening schools is determined primarily by the character of the population in different sections of the city and the extent to which the people living in the neighborhood make

* The need for a wider distribution of evening high schools is recognized in the report on evening schools for the year ending July 31, 1912, and it is recommended "that evening high school 'annexes' consisting of two or more first-year classes be established in elementary evening school buildings in sections of the city too far removed from the main building, that such classes maintain an organization independent of the elementary school, and, if the attendance allows, continue sessions for the full period of 120 evenings." Superintendent of Schools, New York City. Fourteenth Annual Report, 1911–12. Report on Evening Schools for the Year Ending July 31, 1912, p. 44.

use of the schools. The very atmosphere of the streets changes as you walk from one district to another.

Thus, in the borough of Manhattan, on the West Side between Fifty-ninth Street and Washington Heights, a district largely inhabited by prosperous residents, the main body of working women are domestic servants whose hours of service do not permit them to be "out" four nights a week. Only two evening schools for women were located in this district, one at the corner of Amsterdam Avenue and Ninety-third Street, the other at St. Nicholas Avenue and 127th Street. Dark desertion at night characterizes certain blocks on the lower West Side, where the streets are lined with closed warehouses and dingy tenements which were once fashionable private residences. In block after block one finds stillness and emptiness, accentuated by the footfalls of an occasional passerby. Below Fourteenth Street on the lower West Side, but two small schools were found. One was in an Italian neighborhood and its attendance suffered from the Italian custom of keeping the unmarried daughters at home in the evening. The other stood but a stone's throw from Trinity church and Wall Street, at the corner of Albany, Washington, and Carlisle streets, in a district peopled by heterogeneous groups of Syrians, Greeks, Turks, and Egyptians, with a mixture of various other nationalities.

On the lower East Side, beyond the Bowery,

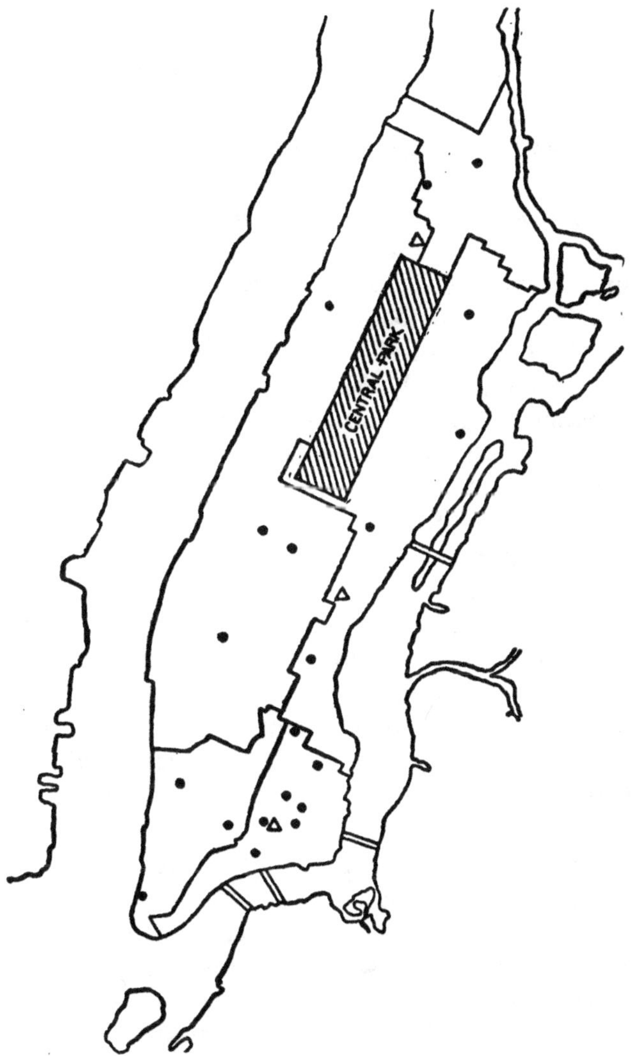

PUBLIC EVENING SCHOOLS FOR WOMEN IN THE BOROUGH OF MANHATTAN, 1910–11

The dots represent evening elementary schools and the triangles, evening high schools.

in contrast, the streets at night are ablaze with light and gay with activity. We seem here to be in another city. Open shops line the way; noisy voices of push-cart peddlers cry their wares; and men, women, and babies crowd the sidewalk. In this neighborhood the evening schools flourish. Of the 50,000 girls and women enrolled in all the schools of the Greater City in the season of 1910–11, nearly 8,000 were in schools south of Houston Street and east of Broadway. Many of the pupils in these schools were Jews, whose desire for scholarship and eagerness for economic advancement bring them to the night schools in large numbers.

No two schools are alike in racial composition. It is these contrasts in nationality, with all the differences that they imply in custom, in tradition, in ideals of education, and early school training, which make the public school system of New York a federation of almost separate educational units instead of a unified, homogeneous institution. In the evening school on the corner of Lexington Avenue and 106th Street, only about one in ten of the girls investigated* were of native parentage, while nearly half were daughters of Russians. In contrast with this was an elementary school on West Twenty-fourth Street, in which only one of the 247 girls who answered our questions reported that father was born in Russia, while 82 fathers were of native and 103 of Irish or English parent-

* Appendix I, Table C, Public School No. 72, p. 192.

age. Or again, the proportion of girls of native-born parentage varied from 1.6 per cent in the evening high school on the lower East Side to 27 per cent in the high school in East Forty-first Street; and from 5.3 per cent in an elementary school in an Italian neighborhood* to 71 per cent in one in West Forty-sixth Street in the midst of a Negro population.

Naturally, the classes in English for foreigners contain only pupils of foreign birth, and here the greatest diversity of nationalities is found. Many have found their way to the schools within a few weeks of their arrival. But it is not only these classes that are attended by pupils of foreign birth. Our records show that many countries are represented, also, in classes in which all the pupils must necessarily be able to understand and speak the language of this country.

It was with the English-speaking girls, whether native or foreign born, that our investigation was primarily concerned, since the method of investigation was to secure written answers in English to questions, and the newly arrived immigrants were not generally able to meet this test. In some cases, however, the teachers of the non-English-speaking classes filled out the cards for their pupils, and in certain of the more advanced classes in the foreign department our record cards were welcomed as an opportunity for presenting an interesting lesson in English. Therefore, it has been difficult in our

* Public School No. 23, Mulberry and Bayard streets.

inquiry to draw a hard and fast line between the foreign department, which we had intended to exclude, and the classes which predominated in our inquiry. In the great majority of cases, however, the women who filled our records could both speak and write English.

Thus, since not many of the pupils in the classes for recent immigrants were included, our information regarding nationality does not represent the whole group of women who attend evening schools. We were aiming rather to get a picture of the working girls who had either been born here, or had been here long enough to be fairly representative of American working conditions, and whose desire for instruction in evening classes was significant in its relation to the problem of industrial education. Table 2 shows the birthplaces of this group of girls in the evening schools.

The majority, 68 per cent, were born in the United States. The next largest group, 16 per cent, were Russians, with 5.1 per cent from Austria-Hungary. Among the Russian-born pupils were Lithuanians, Ruthenians, Poles, and many Jews. A large proportion of the girls who are listed as having been born in Austria and Germany were Polish or Jewish. The small group of other nationalities includes Canadians, French, Spaniards, Greeks, Turks, and Syrians. Some of these foreign-born women had been attending the evening schools for several years. They began in the classes in English, and then, after learning

TABLE 2.—NATIVITY OF WOMEN ATTENDING PUBLIC EVENING SCHOOLS[a]

Country of birth	Women born as specified	
	Number	Per cent
United States	8,907	68.2
Russia	2,034	15.6
Austria-Hungary[b]	660	5.1
Germany	346	2.6
Italy	214	1.6
Ireland	194	1.5
Great Britain	167	1.3
Roumania	160	1.2
Scandinavia	112	.9
Other countries	256	2.0
Total	13,050[c]	100.0

[a] Data for selected occupations in trade and transportation and in manufacturing and mechanical pursuits are given in Appendix I, Table J, p. 201.

[b] Includes Bohemia.

[c] Of the 13,141 women included in the study, 91 did not supply information.

the language, advanced to other courses—millinery or dressmaking, grammar and arithmetic, or even science or literature in the high schools. In some instances they had had schooling in their native land representing more than the equivalent of our high school courses.

Racial traits persist for more than one generation, and thus it is that we have in the evening schools more of Germany, or Italy, or Russia than the statistics quoted in Table 2 would indicate, since many of the American-born girls are the children of foreign parents. Table 3 shows the birthplaces of the fathers of the girls investigated.

TABLE 3.—NATIVITY OF FATHERS OF WOMEN ATTENDING PUBLIC EVENING SCHOOLS[a]

Country of birth	WOMEN WITH FATHERS BORN AS SPECIFIED	
	Number	Per cent
Russia	2,979	23.4
United States	2,908	22.8
Germany	2,133	16.7
Ireland	1,444	11.3
Austria-Hungary[b]	1,360	10.7
Great Britain	539	4.2
Italy	489	3.8
Scandinavia	294	2.3
Roumania	209	1.6
Other countries	413	3.2
Total	12,768[c]	100.0

[a] Data appear for each school in Appendix I, Table C, p. 192.

[b] Includes Bohemia.

[c] Of the 13,141 women included in the study, 373 did not supply information.

The United States occupies a less prominent place in this table than in that showing the birthplaces of the girls themselves. Only 23 per cent of these evening school girls had fathers who were born in this country, while 23 per cent were of Russian parentage, 17 per cent German, and 11 per cent Irish. The birthplaces of the fathers of 11 per cent were in Austria-Hungary. The daughters of Italians number only 3.8 per cent, although in the general population their rank is much higher.

The principal of one of the evening schools on the lower East Side told of the inspiration she had gained from the thoughtful and earnest foreign girls who came to the classes there. A number were alone in this country, meeting the new conditions here independently and with wonderful courage. The preceding year many of them had been leaders in the big strike of shirtwaist makers, but no less important cause could keep them away from class any night in the term. When they had to work overtime in the factories they would come to school straight from work without any dinner. Then they would go home and do their laundry work late at night—the only time when the families with whom they boarded would give them the use of the washtubs. Even after that task the flower or feather makers would spend several hours working on flowers or feathers brought home from the factory. Most of these were Jewish girls from Russia, or Austria, or Germany, eager to learn all they could about America; keen and independent in judgment; and withal, ready to make sacrifices not for themselves alone but for their fellow-workers, to improve the conditions in their trades.

One of the most thoughtful of these women students in the evening high schools was a young Russian milliner who had been in this country six years. She had been observing American conditions and American characteristics as she had seen them in the wholesale millinery shops, in the evening schools, in theaters, and on the streets. Her conversation with the investigator who went to talk with her about the millinery trade covered many subjects,—socialism, woman's rights, trade unions, Bernard Shaw, the drama in America, the school system, and Russian versus American women. She had been an ardent worker in a little band of milliners who had tried to organize a union, but she had given it up as a hopeless task.

"It took time that we might spend on a book, or studying, or going to the theater. And besides, it's no use trying to organize the American women. They don't care about anything but making dates. It's all men and dances, and they don't care about organizing because they expect to get married and stop working. It's no use talking to them. When you begin on unions they call you a Socialist, and that ends it; or if you talk about woman's suffrage, they laugh at you. Why should they laugh?"

She would like to go home to see her parents in Russia, she said. "But I don't think I should want to stay. There is something fascinating about America. But they are not thinkers here. It's all money. They don't think—but then not many people do in any country. American women are not disturbed enough. You have to be disturbed to think. Russian women seem to me to be the finest in the world, and it is because things have been hard for them."

The Italians who find their way into the evening schools are those who have acquired a point of view quite different from that of their nation. For an Italian girl to be away from home at night unattended is to oppose custom and to run the risk of unpleasant gossip in the neighborhood, even though she does not thereby incur the disapproval of her family. Furthermore, the leisure time of the wage-earning Italian girl must usually be spent in some home occupation adding directly or indirectly to the family income, in preparation for the time when she shall be married and require a dot. The object of Italian parents is to marry their daughters well and young, and a marriage portion increases the likelihood of their attaining both these objects. Many a time has one of our investigators met with the kindly and courteous, but pitying, comments of Italian men and women who have marveled at her cheerfulness though still unmarried after the ripe age of twenty-five. This deep-rooted conviction as to the destiny of women leaves no room yet for the thought that prolonged education may be of value to a girl.

Maria, a young Italian wage-earner, wanted to join a class in an evening school very near her home. Her family were so far advanced in their ideas of education that they had paid the tuition of her sister in a business school. Nevertheless, Maria went only a few times, when her father and mother, growing solicitous about this defiance of conventional rules, forbade her being out at night.

Soon afterward she married, and from that time on she went out only to do her marketing, since her husband objected to having her leave the house even during the day. To be discontented did not occur to her. She told the visitor proudly that she was "very pleased" with her husband. Tessa, another Italian girl, actually continued to go to evening school for a winter, but the following year she did not return. She explained that she no longer had time to go out since, after coming home from work in a neckwear factory, she was obliged to wash the dishes and make up all the folding beds for a family of eight.

Others, however, have found the evening classes a great help in their ambition to fashion costumes which might increase their opportunities to get ahead in the world in the traditional Italian way for women. Carmela, a maker of fancy feathers, proudly showed the product of her work in an evening class in dressmaking. It was a pale blue silk gown with a "fish-tail" train, a lace bodice, and a draped tunic. She had made it to wear to a wedding in the neighborhood. She had also contributed to the family resources by making a blue serge dress for her younger sister, thus saving a dressmaker's bill.

While among some races family custom keeps a girl out of evening school, often the ambition of her parents encourages her to "get more education." Sarah, a Russian girl of fifteen, told us that she went because her father, a Hebrew teacher, cautiously advised it, saying, "Education won't hurt you." Margaret, whose Irish father is a motorman for a New York street car line, went regularly to evening high school chiefly because, as her stepmother expressed it, "The father wants to do the best he can for her." He took a keen interest in "Daisy's" schooling, and the stepmother urged the visitor to find out for her how the child was getting along in her classes. "The father often asks her could he go to the school and see the teacher, because we don't get no reports. But Daisy says nobody can do that. We'd like to know if she's doing well."

Florence was a messenger in a New York department store. It was her mother, an Irishwoman, who encouraged her to go regularly to evening school. She wanted her to get more education, and then perhaps the family could spare a little money later to train her in stenography so that she could have better work than the store seemed likely to offer. Her mother had wanted her to graduate from day school, but just as she was within one term of it she failed of promotion. "I felt awful bad about it," said her mother. "I went to the teacher and the teacher said she was lazy and better be put to work. She asked me didn't I notice the reports that Florence was poor in arithmetic. I come home and scolded the father that he hadn't paid more attention to it. He was born in New York and went to school here, but I wasn't. I came here when I was fourteen and what education I've had I got from reading newspapers and picking it up any way I could. I want my daughters to be educated."

AGES OF EVENING SCHOOL STUDENTS

The opportunity afforded the evening schools for adding to the meager schooling many of these American girls have had, and for interpreting America to workers of foreign parentage and bringing about a better understanding between women of different races is the greater because of the youth of the pupils in the classes. In the year 1911–12, 8,825 women of twenty-one years or older were registered in the elementary schools, as compared with 25,238 girls under twenty-one.* In the high schools the women numbered 3,949 and the girls, 9,294.† Table 4 shows the ages of the women and girls included in this investigation.

One in five was under sixteen and 32 per cent, nearly one-third, were between sixteen and eighteen. Only 23 per cent had passed the twenty-first birthday. The figures just quoted for all the women and girls registered in the elementary and high schools in 1911–12 showed that 27 per cent, 12,774, were twenty-one or older. The slight difference between this proportion and that of our

* Superintendent of Schools, New York City. Fourteenth Annual Report, 1911–12. Report on Evening Schools for the Year Ending July 31, 1912, p. 16.

In the report for the year ending July 31, 1911, the statistics according to age are not given.

† Ibid., p. 45. In the evening trade schools 452 girls and 459 women were registered.

group in the preceding year is probably due to the fact that in the classes in English for foreigners not included by us, the pupils, many of whom have come alone to this country, are older than in the other classes.*

TABLE 4.—AGES OF WOMEN ATTENDING PUBLIC EVENING SCHOOLS[a]

Age	WOMEN OF THE AGES SPECIFIED	
	Number	Per cent
Less than 16 years	2,632	20.3
16 years and less than 18 years . . .	4,184	32.2
18 years and less than 21 years . . .	3,128	24.1
21 years or more	3,043	23.4
Total	12,987[b]	100.0

[a] Data appear by principal occupational groups and for selected occupations in Appendix I, Table G, p. 198, and by selected occupations in trade and transportation and in manufacturing and mechanical pursuits in Appendix I, Table J, p. 201.

[b] Of the 13,141 women included in the study, 154 did not supply information.

THE PUPILS' AIMS

It is characteristic of evening school pupils that they have joined a class with a practical end in view. They wish to learn English, to study Spanish

* Of the whole group, 931, or 7.1 per cent of the 13,141, were married or widowed. The proportion of married women and widows in the group of non-wage-earners was 21.2 per cent, or larger than among the wage-earners, of whom only 2.2 per cent were or had been married. In manufacturing and mechanical pursuits the proportion was only 1.5 per cent; in trade and transportation, 1 per cent; in professional work, 5.2 per cent; and in domestic and personal service, 16.3 per cent.

in order to qualify as stenographers in commercial houses with branches in Cuba or Porto Rico, to make a hat for Easter, to learn to cook in preparation for marriage and housekeeping, or, if the aim be general education, to secure a foundation for later training for some more attractive occupation than the one at present followed. Among the girls included in our study, the popularity of academic subjects, commercial courses, and classes in hand work was about equal; 32 per cent were in manual classes, 31 per cent in academic, 31 per cent in commercial courses, with a scattered few who were studying art or elocution. Ten per cent were enrolled in English classes. In some cases the same girl was studying an academic subject one hour and a commercial subject the second, thus being counted in both groups.

The girls' motives for joining evening classes are interesting. In the course of our visits to their homes, 271 were asked why they attended night school. Table 5 gives their answers.

Obviously, in analyzing the girls' reasons for coming to evening school, we must remember that in a sense these will be determined by what the evening schools now have to offer. At present it is not likely that a girl employed, for example, in a paper box factory or a bookbindery would say that she was enrolled in an evening class in order to improve her earning capacity in her day's work. The less the emphasis upon vocational training in the schools, the less prominent will be the vocational

STUDYING "COMMON BRANCHES"
Making up deficiencies

COOKING CLASS

motive in the minds of the pupils. Extension of trade classes would doubtless result in a great change in motives for attending. At present, if the group interviewed be typical, three aims rival

TABLE 5.—REASONS GIVEN BY 271 WOMEN FOR ENROLLING IN PUBLIC EVENING SCHOOLS

Reason	Women who enrolled for each specified reason
In order to change to better work	75
To learn for "home use"	74
To obtain a general education	72
To help in daily occupation	25
Went with friends	8
Thought the law required attendance	6
"Nothing else to do"	4
To prepare for positions that were offered	2
To keep up speed in stenography while not at work	1
"Mother made her go"	1
Sent by father "to keep her off the streets"	1
Acquaintance with teacher	1
"Just happened to go"	1
Total	271 [a]

[a] Of the 13,141 women included in the study, 271 were questioned as to their reasons for attending public evening school. Of these 271 women, 201 were in evening elementary schools and 70 in evening high schools.

one another in importance,—"home use," as illustrated by the married woman who enters a dressmaking class to learn how to make her children's clothes; "general education," as revealed in the case of the stock girl in a department store who had joined a class in "common branches" in order, as she said, "to finish the subjects I didn't finish in day school"; and "to change to better work," an indication of the discontent felt by many girls who have a great desire to learn a new trade to enable them to make a fresh start.

Of the need for finishing what was not finished in day school, the spelling on the record cards is a convincing sign. The worker on "ledes dresses" was rivaled in orthographic ingenuity by the girl who made "papar bocses." The "wilomaker" was a match for the "toker,"—words which, being interpreted, stand for willow-maker and tucker. "Exzamining" is entirely intelligible, if not Websterian, as is also "Ladie's underware." The word operator provided an exercise in versatility. It appeared impartially as aprether, apertergn, upraitter, apreder, aperater, apraider, ipratair, aperiter, apeirder, opereider, oposeter, aprading, opprerate, opertor, apreider, and opparating. The phonetic method was revealed in the writing of a girl who had reached the 6B grade after eight years in a New York public school. She had been out of work "2 ears" and was now trying to make good her deficiencies in arithmetic and geography by joining an evening class whose subjects, as far as she was concerned, went by the name of "erefnret" and "girgofrie." A girl who had attended New York public schools eight and a half years, reaching the 8B grade, wrote that she was now employed in a "book boundary." Another, who had attained the 8A grade in an elementary school, described her occupation as "Book binind" and said that her father was born in "Irland." One girl was employed in a "deportment store" and another called herself a "sail lady."

Defective spelling does not always yield to treatment and is not always indicative of a lack of general intelligence, but it is not unreasonable to expect that a girl shall know how to spell the name of her occupation. Undoubtedly, however, the spelling books have not kept pace with industrial development. In the interests of industrial education they should be brought up to date in this respect.

For many of these girls the enrollment in an evening class in 1910 was not their first effort to add to their educational equipment. Two thousand of the 13,000 investigated had previously attended the evening elementary schools and 1,100 the evening high schools. Eighteen hundred had had courses in private business schools and a small group of 241 had attended trade schools. That is, 4,902, or 37 per cent of the women investigated, had already proved their desire for additional training by joining some special class since leaving day school.

Evening classes are not new in the public school system. They were organized in New York as early as 1847, and their primary purpose throughout their history has been to meet the educational needs of wage-earners. In early years, however, emphasis was placed on general education for "the enlightenment of ignorance." The schools were described as part of "a great crusade against ignorance or vice," and as safeguards against the temptations encountered by young girls and boys who otherwise would spend their evenings on the streets. The present-day interest in industrial education is having an influence on evening schools by changing the conception of the educational needs of wage-earners. School authorities are talking now not so much about a crusade against ignorance as about plans to give definite instruction directed toward increasing the skill of workers.

The problem of giving instruction to increase skill in various occupations is not an easy one for either day schools or evening schools to handle. The first difficulty in the way is the lack of adequate information regarding industrial conditions. Obviously, if the schools are to meet the needs of working women, the teachers, and principals, and all who have anything to do with planning or carrying out the curriculum, must know in detail the occupations which employ girls. They must understand the processes into which trades are divided; the training required for them; the standards of wages, hours, and sanitation generally prevailing; the need of the workers for a broader view of their own tasks and of their social and industrial relations; and the methods of co-operation which may be possible between school, employer, and worker. To answer these questions thoroughly it would be necessary to make intensive studies of each industry. As a basis for such thorough study, however, it is valuable to know certain facts about the large number of working girls already seeking more education in evening schools.

MAIN GROUPS OF OCCUPATIONS

How many and varied are the occupations now represented in the evening schools of New York will be revealed in later chapters. At this point it is desirable to know the proportion employed in the main groups of wage-earning pursuits. Table 6 states these facts for the girls included in our investigation.

TABLE 6.—DAILY OCCUPATIONS OF WOMEN ATTENDING PUBLIC EVENING SCHOOLS, BY PRINCIPAL OCCUPATIONAL GROUPS

Principal occupational group	WOMEN EMPLOYED AS SPECIFIED	
	Number	Per cent
Manufacturing and mechanical pursuits	4,519	34.4
Trade and transportation	4,505	34.3
Domestic and personal service	520	4.0
Professional service	193	1.5
No occupation stated [a]	3,404	25.8
Total	13,141	100.0

[a] When the questions relating to daily occupations were not answered, it was assumed that the women were not gainfully employed. Visits to a few of them indicated that the assumption was correct. The women, therefore, who are included in the group with no occupation stated, are considered throughout the report as not gainfully employed. For further explanation, see footnote, p. 36.

The phrases used to describe these occupational groups are familiar to students of the United States Census. Manufacturing and mechanical pursuits include all factory work. "Trade and transportation" refers not to trades, as might be supposed, but to many diverse tasks which have to do with trading or selling goods to customers. In this group, which is second to factory work as an occupation chosen by evening school girls, are included all who work in telegraph or telephone exchanges, and those employed in stores or offices as saleswomen, stenographers, bookkeepers, clerical workers, and the like.

The proportion of non-wage-earners, 26 per cent, shown in Table 6, may seem surprising.* It should be remembered, however, that women who are not earning money are in the majority in New York. Of every four women in the city three are not working for wages, while in the evening schools this proportion is exactly reversed, thus indicating that the schools appeal primarily to the working women in the community.

The proportion of non-wage-earners in the

* As the table shows, 3,404 made no report on occupation. In some instances this may have been merely a careless failure to answer the question; but in the majority of cases the remainder of the record was sufficiently full to justify the conclusion that the greater number of these girls were not wage-earners. Further, as shown by the card given in the Appendix, p. 186, we asked not only "What is the business of the firm for which you now work?" but "If out of work at present, what was the business of the firm for which you last worked?" Only those who answered neither of these questions were counted in the group "No occupation stated." The number who answered the second, thus reporting themselves as out of work, was small,—only 536, or 5.5 per cent of the wage-earners who filled the record cards.

schools varies in different sections of the city. In Manhattan and the Bronx they numbered 19 per cent and in Brooklyn, 35 per cent. In school No. 10 in the Bronx the proportion was 37 per cent as compared with only 5.6 per cent not at work in school No. 177 on the lower East Side. Quite as marked are the variations in different schools in the proportion of workers in each occupational group.

Within the walls of school buildings in New York, then, every night when evening schools are in session are to be found pupils of many nationalities and diverse occupations. The national groupings are to a certain degree peculiar to New York. Splendid material is found among the foreign-born adult pupils. In the spirit of a great people's university the public schools in the evening should be made a center for an interchange of thought and idealism to which each race may contribute its best. The teachers must concern themselves also with vocational problems, which are significant not for New York only, but for every city in which modern industrial conditions are complex. Everywhere the schools are hard-pressed to find the answers to many questions forced upon their attention by changing conditions. Especially urgent and puzzling are those which concern the education of wage-earning women and girls.

CHAPTER II

OCCUPATIONS OF GIRLS WHO GO TO NIGHT SCHOOL

EVERYONE knows that great changes have taken place in women's work in the past fifty years. Few understand the diversity of these changes, nor do they realize how numerous and varied are the tasks by which women and girls now try to earn their living. The girls who gather in the evening schools have come from office, factory, or store. During their working day they have been answering the incessant calls for "central" or for "cash girl"; they have been goffering rose leaves with a hot iron, rolling cigarettes, putting labels on cigars by the thousands or olives into glass bottles, feeding the ten thousandth sheet into a folding machine in a book bindery, typewriting office letters, selling "notions," testing electric light bulbs in a dark room, stitching hundreds of yards of ruffling on power machines, trimming hats, or draping fashionable gowns. A long and varied list of occupations, with a high grade of skill required for a few, but with endless monotony characteristic of many of them,—this is the modern industrial world for women which challenges attention not only in evening schools but in all branches of the educational system.

As early as 1858 the board of education of New York City called attention to the changing conditions of women's work and the need for industrial education. The annual report* of that year estimates "that no less than 80,000 females are engaged in various occupations, mostly in the manufactories which are found in various parts of our city."

"Very little opportunity," the report continues, "is afforded to them for purposes of study, and it is not therefore surprising that of this vast number the comparatively few who enter our evening schools are in the lower classes. During the past year the improvements made in the sewing machines have rendered them so perfect that they have been in many cases substituted for female labor, thereby throwing large numbers of females out of employment. This has been felt by them to be a very serious evil, as other branches of female labor seem to have as many employed in them as can well be accommodated. What, therefore, can be done for this unfortunate class of our population?

"Your committee believe that the time is rapidly approaching when the male clerks in most of our retail stores will be exchanged for females, who are so well adapted to fill such positions. Already very many employers have secured the services of this class and feel well satisfied with the exchange.

"That they may be qualified in every respect to discharge faithfully and successfully the duties apper-

* New York Board of Education. Annual Report, 1858, p. 189.

taining to these positions, it is necessary that they should possess a thorough knowledge of accounts and some familiarity with the elements of bookkeeping. Our evening schools are competent to impart this desirable information, and we urge upon all who wish to obtain situations as clerks in stores to avail themselves of the facilities which are now so favorably presented to them."

More than fifty years have elapsed since these words were written, and few of the thousands of girls in the sewing trades in New York now know that the rapid, whirring machines which need so many operators ever threw any women out of work, and the long lines of salesgirls in the huge modern department stores would be even more surprised to hear that the board of education had once offered courses to enable displaced seamstresses to fill the positions of male retail clerks, in the hope that some day many more women might find that occupation open to them.

That wish of 1858 has been amply fulfilled. The census of 1900 told us that in the house-to-house canvass, enumerators found 65,318 girls in Greater New York employed in "trade and transportation," which includes salesgirls, bookkeepers, stenographers, office clerks, and all others engaged in the business of selling or transporting goods after their manufacture. But these occupations do not appear to have taken the place of sewing or any other form of manual work, for the same census reported 132,535 women in manufacturing establishments. Of the 169,584 other wage-earning women in New York, 146,722 were in domestic or personal service, 22,422 in professional service, and 440 in agriculture.*

CHANGES IN WOMEN'S WORK

Technical and cumbersome as the census classification may seem, in its setting of many statistics, it is merely an official description of the modern way of satisfying our social and physical needs. Fundamentally, not the needs but the methods of supplying them have changed. Food, shelter, clothing, and social intercourse,—these are the necessities of life for which men and women have always labored. For modern workers, however, the terms of the day's labor are different. Today we have a long list of occupations grouped under five large heads: mining and agriculture, representing the extraction of raw food and materials from the earth; manufacturing and mechanical pursuits, including all the tasks of preparing for sale innumerable articles of food, shelter, clothing, and luxury; trade and transportation, with all the diverse schemes of organization necessary to transport goods from place to place, and finally, to consummate a sale; professional service, which corresponds roughly to the need which we have defined as social intercourse, including law and government, science, medicine, art, and teaching; and, fifth in these large groups of occupations,

* Twelfth United States Census, 1900. Special Reports, Occupations, p. 640. For figures from the census of 1910, see this volume, p. 183.

domestic and personal service, embracing alike the service rendered in households by maids to mistresses and the more highly organized tasks of cooks and waiters in a hotel, of hairdressers and manicures, office cleaners, and janitors.

This last group brings into prominence the fact that the economic world is still in a state of transition. The methods of performing many tasks are highly organized; while others are still carried on in private households. A great deal of work is paid for under the wage system; while often the worker spends her energies in meeting her own needs or the needs of her family, and receives no money in return. Doubtless many of the evening school pupils whom we have classified as non-wage-earners were productive workers at home in tasks not paid for in wages. In such a transitional period it is natural that public opinion should grow confused on the subject of women's work. Her employment outside the home is spoken of as a new and abnormal phenomenon, while certain tasks, like domestic service, or dressmaking, or millinery have always been considered her normal occupation, even when carried on elsewhere than in the home. Perhaps this confusion about woman's sphere is due to an inability to see the process of change and to face the fact that women are experiencing not an enlargement of their field of work but a violent revolution in the method of doing it.

This process has gone on for the most part unnoticed, and not until millions of women had joined the ranks of wage-earners in this country did the general public begin to realize its portentous character. Even now, in many a city, the majority of the population have but a vague impression of the nature and conditions of industries carried on at their very doors. It was in 1907 that "the first general survey of the women-employing trades of an American city" was undertaken.* Curiously enough, Pittsburgh was the scene of the investigation—a fact which emphasizes the difference between actual conditions and the public impression of them. For the industries of Pittsburgh, even in the minds of Pittsburghers, are not of the feminine type, and as Miss Butler points out in the opening sentences of her report: "Pittsburgh as a workshop for women seems a contradiction in terms." Mines and steel works, the digging of crude ores, and the fusing and forging of them,† do not require women's work. In the city in which these tremendous operations compel attention, it is only the thoughtful and observant who are aware of the more humdrum work necessary to satisfy the needs of a large laboring population. It is precisely because the work of women is often concerned with needs which are not new and therefore are taken

* The investigation was made by Miss Elizabeth B. Butler as part of the Pittsburgh Survey, under the direction of Charities Publication Committee with the co-operation of the Russell Sage Foundation. The results were published as the first volume of the Pittsburgh Survey Series,—Butler, Elizabeth B.: Women and the Trades. Russell Sage Foundation Publication. New York, Charities Publication Committee, 1910.

† Yet the women chain makers of England set up little forges in their own homes, and there hammer out the links.

for granted without further thought, that the changed conditions of their work are so little understood.

The women workers in the city of mines and steel works were employed in food production, in the stogy industry,—fulfilling the workingman's wish for a cheap smoke,—in the needle trades, in saleswork, in telephone operating, and in the cleaning industries,—important in a city of smoke and grime. Nothing very unusual or very dramatic appears in that enumeration, but interest is aroused when we are given more details of the picture. It is not commonplace to find "women molding metals, shaping lamps, and making glass," "girl thread makers at the screw and bolt works," and "strong-armed women who fashion sand cores in foundries planned like Alberich's smithy in the underworld." Even "the hill-dwelling wives of the miners" had not escaped the modern demands of industry, since their wooden shacks had become sweatshops to which the garment factories sent out work to be done for a pittance.

Slavic girls and women, sisters and wives of mill workers, are to be found in canneries and cracker factories where they "pack or fill jars at high speed." In tin plate mills they "open the sheets of tin, still warm from the furnaces. They screw nuts or bolts by a fish-oil process, and carry heavy trays in foundries where they have displaced men. They are the packers in glass factories, the riveters and foot-press operators in lamp works."

Chivalry has not made easy the way of women in industry, nor have the lighter tasks always been accorded to them. Neither have they met with fair play in the terms of the labor bargain. Miss Butler thus sums up her picture: "Many of these women are put to work at wages below the cost of subsistence, for hours longer than the measure of their strength, in buildings and at ill-constructed machines which can not but injure their health, and at processes which must handicap heavily the development of both mind and body."*

What Miss Butler did that year for Pittsburgh the Department of Commerce and Labor was beginning in 1907 to undertake for the whole country with its 5,000,000 women workers. Nineteen volumes contain the findings submitted to Congress.† They show that the condition in Pittsburgh is essentially characteristic of many other communities. The government investigators followed women into the glass factories of 17 states and watched them sorting and packing the ware, chipping and filing the necks of bottles, glazing, etching, and decorating glassware. They found them in the cotton mills tending the big machines and engaged in a variety of minute processes, in air so heated and moist as to be good for the cotton but bad for the women and children employed. In the metal trades of 13 states women were impor-

* Butler, op. cit., p. 28.

† Report on the Condition of Woman and Child Wage-Earners in the United States. Senate Document No. 645.

tant factors. They fed bolts into the presses "at considerable risk" of injury to their hands. As in Pittsburgh, so in many other cities, girls were making the sand cores for the casting of brassware. In the manufacture of firearms and ammunition they were polishing gun barrels and assembling locks. They were tending machines for making tin cans, an industry in which, the report says, the "accident rate among women is very high."

These are but stray illustrations of the material presented in this nineteen-volume government report. The material itself is but a series of views of women at work in certain occupations and communities selected for investigation. No large city was completely surveyed. Many industrial communities were omitted for lack of time and money to study them.

DIVERSE OCCUPATIONS AMONG EVENING SCHOOL PUPILS

That New York City is a mirror for the industries of the whole country is vividly demonstrated in the variety of occupations represented in the evening schools. As already shown in the first chapter, of the 13,141 girls who filled record cards in the investigation on which these chapters are based, 4,519 were employed in manufacturing, 4,505 in trade and transportation, 193 in professions, and 520 in domestic and personal service.

So diverse are the occupations within these different groups that the mere naming and classifying of them presents a problem which is at present puzzling even experts in the census bureau of the United States. Manufacturing, for example, defies attempts at classification. Shall workers be grouped according to the actual process in which they are engaged, or according to the product of their industry? If we count all who take part in the making of dresses as dressmakers, we have the girl who cuts out embroidery in a large wholesale factory for ready-made clothing counted with the draper in a fashionable Fifth Avenue custom shop. Such a classification would throw light on the number engaged in the dressmaking industry, but tell us nothing about the relative skill or position of the workers. On the other hand, if we should count all machine operators together, we should have those who make bathing suits or shirtwaists, for instance, classed with those who sew straw hats, or flour sacks, or window shades; and the number would not be significant either as indicating those engaged in separate industries, or as an enumeration of a group of workers encountering similar conditions. Furthermore, any such plan would make comparison with official figures impossible, as hitherto the basis of classification by the census and the New York State Department of Labor has been the product, not the process. In grouping the evening school pupils according to their occupations, we have, therefore, classified those in manufacturing according to the product, following as closely as possible the grouping adopted by the New York State Department of Labor.*

The women who were counted as employed in manufacturing and mechanical pursuits were really at work in nine large industries with 82 distinct divisions. When we realize that these 82 minor divisions include such important separate trades as shirtwaist making and bookbinding, and that within these trades are many distinct occupations, we begin to realize that the field of women's work in New York is neither simple nor homogeneous. The nine large manufacturing groups† represented among the occupations of girls in evening schools are shown in Table 7.

Thus women who attend the evening schools in New York are employed not only in sewing, but in printing and in the manufacture of paper goods. They are not only milliners and artificial flower makers, but workers in the preparation of confectionery, food, tobacco, and bakery products, and in the manufacture of goods of fur, leather, rubber, and hair. In the textile industries they are employed in making articles of flax, hemp, or jute, as well as in fashioning braids, passementerie, laces, or veils. The group called "other occupations in manufacturing and mechanical pursuits" includes work on stone, glass, metal, and precious stones, electrical supplies, articles of wood and

* New York State Department of Labor. Annual Report on Factory Inspection, 1910, pp. 361-374.

† The 82 minor subdivisions of these large industries are shown in Appendix I, Table D, p. 193.

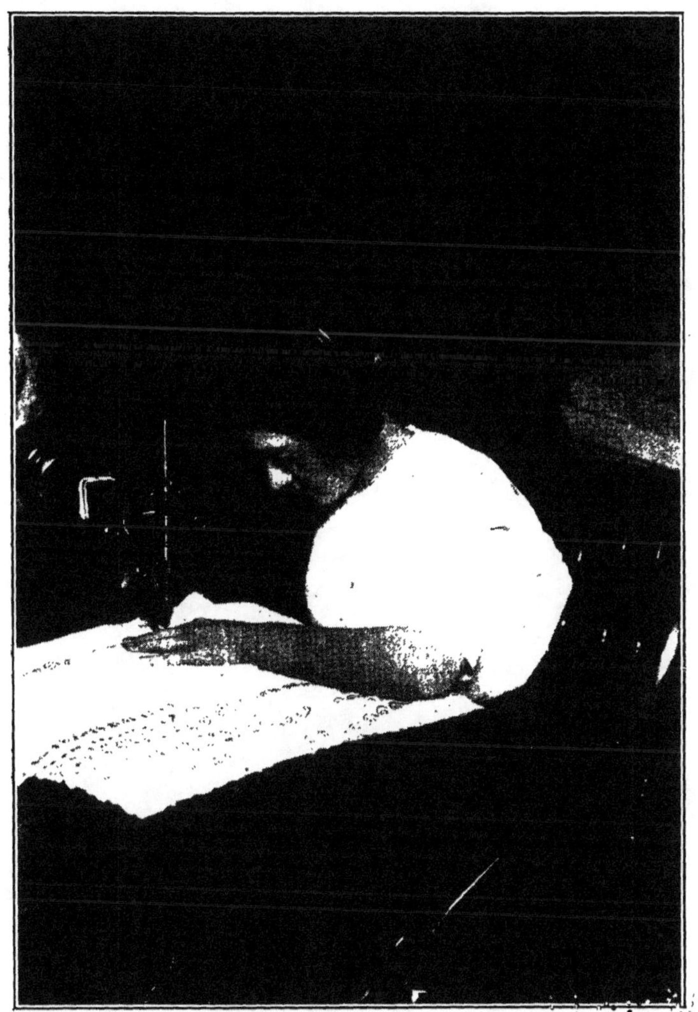

Learning Bonnaz Embroidery

cork, paints and dyes, drugs and chemicals, soap and perfumery, and lamp shades. Here also are counted the laundry workers and the girls employed in establishments for cleaning and dyeing.

TABLE 7.—OCCUPATIONS OF WOMEN ATTENDING PUBLIC EVENING SCHOOLS, EMPLOYED IN MANUFACTURING AND MECHANICAL PURSUITS, BY MAIN GROUPS OF OCCUPATIONS[a]

Occupation	WOMEN EMPLOYED AS SPECIFIED	
	Number	Per cent
Artificial flower and feather making	292	6.5
Making of men's clothing	211	4.7
Making of women's clothing	1,928	42.7
Work on confectionery, food, tobacco, etc.	234	5.2
Work on fur, leather, rubber, hair goods, etc.	344	7.6
Millinery	263	5.8
Miscellaneous needlework	232	5.1
Work on printing and paper goods	417	9.2
Work on textiles	293	6.5
Other occupations in manufacturing and mechanical pursuits	305	6.7
Total	4,519	100.0

[a] Data appear in detail in Appendix I, Table D, p. 193.

The list of these industries is based on the girls' answers to the question: What is the business of the firm for which you now work? Their answers to the question: What work do you do for this firm? tell the story of subdivided tasks. Roughly, these latter classify into tasks of supervision and management; into major processes of manufacture; minor processes of preparation of goods for sale, such as labeling or counting, and odd jobs about the workrooms. For example, in the manufacture of bakery products they did not cook, as some who are unfamiliar with a modern bakery might expect, but they merely packed and labeled, minor tasks which fall to the lot of women in many large industries. In neckwear factories they were designers, operators, trimmers, bow makers, plaiters, lace-runners, preparers, finishers, embroiderers, packers, and floor girls. In shoe making they reported such diverse processes as perforating, buttonhole operating, back strapping, making linings, fitting vamps, marking leather, cleaning, beading, and the inevitable marking and labeling, wrapping and packing. In the tobacco industry they made and stamped cigars; stripped, bunched and rolled cigarettes; fed cigarette machines, boxed, and counted coupons.

This outline of manufacturing and mechanical pursuits does not exhaust the list of women's occupations. Obviously, after goods have been manufactured they must be sold. It will be recalled that the census calls this process, with all its ramifications, "trade and transportation." Table 8 shows the subdivisions in which evening school girls were at work.

The work of the evening school girls in this group includes stenography, bookkeeping and other clerical work, telephone operating, telegraphy, operating adding machines, proofreading, compiling statistics in manufacturing establishments, serving as cashiers in grocery or butcher shops, buying, shopping, and taking part in various processes of selling goods over the counters of stores.

TABLE 8.—OCCUPATIONS OF WOMEN ATTENDING PUBLIC EVENING SCHOOLS AND EMPLOYED IN TRADE AND TRANSPORTATION

Occupation	WOMEN EMPLOYED AS SPECIFIED	
	Number	Per cent
Stenographers and bookkeepers	1,813	40.3
Clerks and office workers	1,754	38.9
Employes in stores including saleswomen, packers, cashiers, stock keepers, messengers, etc.	709	15.7
Stock keepers (other than in department stores)	117	2.6
Cashiers (other than in department stores)	56	1.2
Buyers, shoppers	36	.8
Proofreaders, copy holders	13	.3
Miscellaneous (collectors, agents, etc.)	7	.2
Total	4,505	100.0

The largest group of wage-earning girls in New York is in domestic and personal service, but among evening school pupils representatives of this group are few in numbers. Principals of evening schools cite cases of girls employed in household work who have not been able to continue in classes, even when they made a beginning. The nature of their tasks keeps them on duty longer hours than are required of workers in any factories, stores, or offices in New York. In view of this fact, not the absence of domestic workers, but the number of them in night schools is surprising. But the group of evening school pupils employed in "domestic and personal service" consists not only of maids, cooks, waitresses, and laundresses in private families, but also of office cleaners, janitresses, hairdressers, masseuses, trained nurses, and companions, as well as employes in hotels, restaurants, diet kitchens, and institutions. One pupil was an embalmer in an undertaking establishment.

Finally, there is the small group of professional workers who attend evening classes. These are teachers, governesses, musicians, librarians, interpreters, dietitians, theatrical employes, models, statisticians, and investigators.

A comparison of the occupational grouping of girls enrolled in evening schools with the census figures showing the occupational grouping of working women in the whole population, is necessary to afford a basis for judging whether the public evening schools attract typical working women, and whether the material which we have gathered from the schools may safely be regarded as indicative of the conditions of women's work in New York. The results of this comparison are shown in the accompanying diagram.

Domestic and personal service and the professions are not, as we have indicated, widely represented in the evening schools. These draw their pupils chiefly from the groups engaged in manufacturing and mechanical pursuits, and trade and transportation, with a larger proportion from

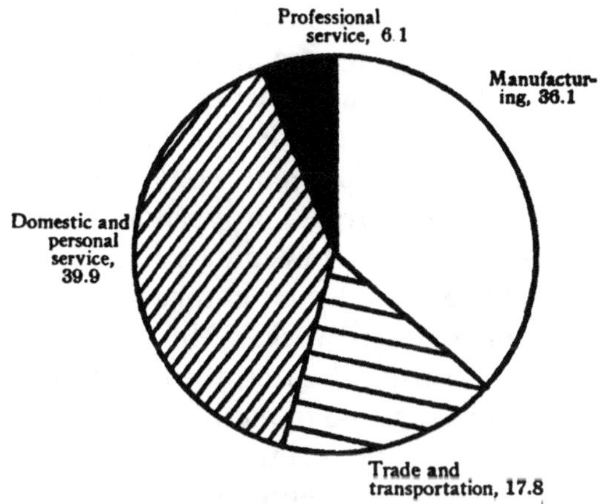

General Population, 1900 [a]

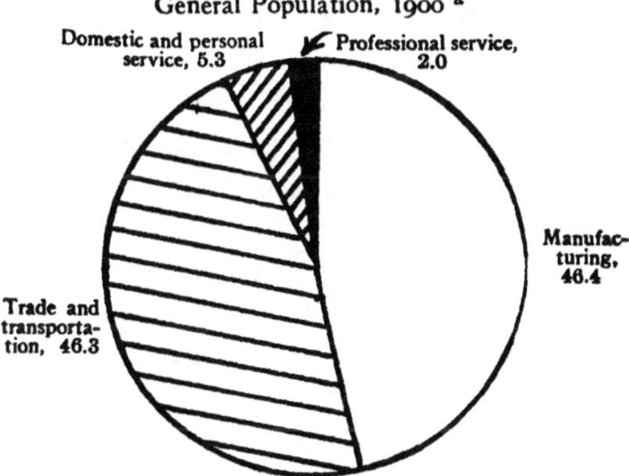

Evening Schools, 1910-11

Diagram I.—Percentage Distribution, by Main Groups of Occupations, of the 367,437 Women Gainfully Employed in New York City as Shown by the Census of 1900, and of 9,737 Women in Public Evening Schools in 1910-11

[a] Of the 367,437 women gainfully employed, 440, or 1 per cent, were employed in "agriculture." This proportion is too small to be represented on the diagram. For figures from the census of 1910, see this volume, p. 183.

trade and transportation than the actual numerical importance of this group among women's occupations in New York would warrant. Perhaps it is natural to suppose that girls engaged in clerical work and similar employment would be found in evening schools in larger proportion than the factory workers, since our evening schools, like our day schools, have placed their emphasis on clerical rather than on manual work. Moreover, as will be seen in the following chapter, the hours in offices are shorter than are those in factories.

Within the manufacturing group in evening classes we have noted representatives of every important trade listed in the census as employing women. Furthermore, the relative importance of the various trades is much the same in evening schools as in the general population. We must make allowance here for the difficulties of classification and the probable differences between our grouping and that of the census. Of the data recorded in the census, the occupational statistics secured from the house-to-house canvass bear the closest resemblance to our investigation in method of inquiry, since both are based on the worker's answer to the general question: What is your occupation? Using these occupational statistics from the census, therefore, and ranking the trade according to its numerical importance among all women employed in this group in 1900 in New York City, and among evening school pupils in 1910, we have the results shown in Table 9.

TABLE 9.—PRINCIPAL OCCUPATIONS IN MANUFACTURING AND MECHANICAL PURSUITS, RANKED ACCORDING TO NUMBER OF WOMEN EMPLOYED, FOR WOMEN ATTENDING PUBLIC EVENING SCHOOLS, 1910-1911, AND FOR ALL WOMEN IN NEW YORK CITY IN 1900

Occupation	RANK OF EACH SPECIFIED OCCUPATION ACCORDING TO NUMBER OF WOMEN EMPLOYED, FOR	
	Women attending public evening schools	All women[a]
Dressmakers and seamstresses	1	1
Tailoresses on men's and women's clothing, including vest makers	2	2
Artificial flower and feather makers	3	10
Milliners	4	3
Embroidery and lace makers	5	7
Bookbinders	6	5
Paper box makers	7	6
Makers of women's neckwear	8	..[b]
Tobacco and cigar factory operatives	9	4
Confectioners	10	12
Workers on knit goods	11	26
Workers on silk goods	12	8
Workers on hair goods	13	..[b]
Metal workers	14	..[b]
Shirt, collar, and cuff makers	15	11

[a] Based on figures in Twelfth United States Census, 1900. Special Reports, Occupations, p. 640.

[b] Not listed separately in the census.

The fact that the census computation for New York City is of a period ten years prior to our investigation* probably accounts for some of the differences in the rank of occupations which may have grown rapidly in the past decade. Three of the groups of trades named in the evening school records are not separately mentioned in the census, —women's neckwear, hair goods, and metal work, —so comparison is not possible in these cases. Cigar making as an occupation ranks ninth in the evening schools and fourth in New York City. In the case of such a trade a reasonable explanation of the small attendance of workers may be found in the long hours commonly prevailing in the industry, and the unhealthy conditions in the workrooms. Thus the proportion from this trade would be lower than among the working population of the city. If, however, we compare the rank of the more important groups,—dressmakers and seamstresses, tailoresses, milliners, bookbinders, paper box makers, and confectionery workers,—the similarity to the census is so marked as to point to the conclusion that on the whole from the point of view of occupational grouping the evening school pupils are representative of women engaged in manufacturing in the city.

This belief has been strengthened by the description of the processes of work carried on by these girls in their trades, and the guide which this gives us in estimating their rank in their

* Early in 1914, the occupational statistics gathered in the census of 1910 were not yet available, because of the inadequate appropriation made by Congress for the necessary work of tabulating and publishing census material.

occupations. It has been seen that workers of various degrees of skill and lack of skill are represented. For example, from "owner" of a dressmaking establishment to "learner," all grades of the industry appear to be included. In view of all these considerations, it seems safe to say that the industrial conditions described by the girls in the evening schools whose occupations brought them under the classification of workers in trade and transportation, and in manufacturing and mechanical pursuits are fairly representative of the industrial conditions of wage-earning women in the largest industrial center in the United States.

FACTS SIGNIFICANT FOR THE SCHOOLS

For educators who wish to equip girls for industry the facts obtained on these 13,000 cards are significant as giving a picture of the kind of work ahead of the thousands of young girls who leave school every year to go to work. Perhaps the most important fact to note is that these evening school girls were employed in at least one process in all but three of the 12 large industrial groups listed by the New York State Department of Labor:* and these three were the manufacture of paper and pulp, as distinct from the making of goods of paper; the building industry; and occupations concerned with supplying water, light, and power in cities and villages. As a corollary, it is

* New York State Department of Labor. Annual Report on Factory Inspection, 1910, p. 361.

obvious that industrial education for women can not be confined to the so-called traditional pursuits of women, such as sewing and cooking, if the movement is to touch the real problems of wage-earning women.

Important also for the schools is a fact which stands out conspicuously in a study of these records,—that apparently work is so organized that in innumerable processes no skill is required. If it be true that the thing which is lacking is not merely a skilled worker, but an opportunity to use skill, then the schools have a larger problem than that of giving technical efficiency to their pupils. In some way they must supply what the industry does not demand, such an all-round development as shall keep alive the general intelligence of the worker. It seems unfair to heap criticism upon the schools for not equipping wage-earners for work, when the larger task of equipping boys and girls for citizenship may demand a training quite unrelated to workshop requirements; a training, indeed, which shall offset the influence of the present organization of work.

If the details which we have cited as illustrative of conditions seem to compose a dreary picture, it should be remembered that such is the sum total of the impression made by recent reports, especially those issued by the government. Furthermore, these are the facts which we must face, if conditions are to be improved. Of the many facts which give investigators courage to believe that great changes for the welfare of the workers are about to be accomplished in industry, three may be cited: First, in every industry one finds pioneer employers who are proving day by day the complete practicability of justice, fair play, and healthful surroundings for the workers. To cite one instance, the government investigators described the contrast between two factories producing essentially the same class of hardware goods. In one the accident rate among women was 17 per 100 workers, while in the other, with its more careful covering of revolving belts and its safety attachments on stamping presses, the corresponding rate was only 1.4 per cent.* Second, we have in increasing numbers investigations like that of the government, affording a basis for improvement through a better conscience in industry itself, and through an aroused public opinion, acting through such established forces as labor legislation and public schools. Third, the fact that women have been tried and not found wanting in so great a variety of occupations indicates that we have in them a great potential force for the material service of humanity, if only we can so change conditions as to give free play to that force.

In New York City, of every four women one is a wage-earner; of every four wage-earners one is a woman; and of every 10 women in the population

* Report on Condition of Woman and Child Wage-Earners in the United States. Vol. XI, Employment of Women in the Metal Trades, p. 75. United States Senate Document No. 645.

one works in a factory.* We have traveled a long distance from the days of self-sufficient households, in which all the necessary tasks of feeding, sheltering, and clothing the family were carried on at home. The change has profoundly influenced women's lives. The hope of fifty years ago that more occupations might be open to them has been fulfilled. In many and diverse ways they are seeking to earn a livelihood for themselves and often for others. How to keep the conditions of their work from being harmful to them, and subsequently to the race,—this is the profoundly important matter with which the community must concern itself.

* The total number of females ten years of age and over in the city in 1900 was 1,356,737. Of these, 367,437 (or one in four) were gainfully employed, and 132,535 (or one in ten) were in manufacturing and mechanical pursuits. The total number of persons, male and female, ten years of age and over, gainfully employed, was 1,469,908; and of this number, one in four was a woman. Twelfth United States Census, 1900. Population, Part II, p. 138; and Occupations, pp. 638 ff. For figures from the census of 1910, see this volume, p. 183.

CHAPTER III

DAILY HOURS OF LABOR

WITH the increasingly complex organization of commerce and industry, the length of the working day has become an important labor problem. To shorten it, men and women have gone out on strike at a cost to them in loss of wages which can never be counted. Legislators have passed laws and courts have handed down decisions as to the right of the state to restrict the length of duration of the day's labor. Reformers have pointed out the social consequences of violating the wage-earners' right to leisure. Finally, physiologists have added the word of science that fatigue is a menace to physical well-being, a poisoning of tissue which can be repaired only by rest taken frequently enough to avoid exhaustion.* Meanwhile, a few who argue against the legislative control of hours of labor point to the good old days when the whole household worked from early dawn until after sundown without interference.

These opponents of the new movement forget how greatly time has altered conditions. Specialization has produced monotony. Speed is a new

* See Goldmark, Josephine: Fatigue and Efficiency, p. 13. Russell Sage Foundation Publication. New York, Charities Publication Committee, 1912.

requirement which has completely changed the life of the worker. Machine tenders and hand workers alike find that their efficiency is measured in terms of rapidity. The movement toward shortening the day's labor is an effort to counteract the ill effects of monotony and speed by giving nature a few more hours in every twenty-four to repair the human machinery. It must never be forgotten in a discussion of evening classes that they represent the wage-earner's use of leisure hours, when mind and body alike must be rested and refreshed lest the net result of the day be a loss of physical vitality. The conditions of the day's work and the length of time spent in the workshop actually determine the results to be attained in the class room at night. The most efficient teacher in an evening class is the one who understands the effect of fatigue on mind and body, and can so stimulate attention and inspire interest as to refresh rather than to tire her pupils. To know the facts about hours is obviously important for the evening schools. It is even more important that the community should understand the conditions as they are reflected in the evening classes, so that greater progress may be made in shortening the hours of labor during the day.

A sixteen-year-old girl in a Brooklyn evening school reported that she worked in a box factory from 7:15 in the morning until 5:30 at night, with a half hour for lunch at noon. Her actual working hours were nine and three-quarters a day. She was studying stenography and typewriting four evenings a week. Another girl sixteen years old worked in a stocking factory from 7 a.m. until 7 p.m., with a half hour for lunch, going to night school to learn dressmaking after a workday of eleven and one-half hours. A cashier in a store worked from 7 a.m. to 6 p.m., with an hour at noon, and studied typewriting and English at night. A machine operator in a silk mill worked from 7 to 6 with three-quarters of an hour at noon. In trades like flower and feather making, in which the girls take work home to do at night, the day's work is often continued after evening school.

Moreover, to the hours of labor in the workroom must be added the time spent in transit, if we would gain any conception of the energy needed to attend night classes. This is the way one girl, a floor hand in a petticoat factory, spent her time. She is typical of many others: Her hours were from 8 a.m. to 6 p.m. She left home at 7:10 a.m. In the morning and evening she swept and dusted the workroom. During the day she ran errands in the factory, except in the half hour allowed for lunch. She reached home for dinner at 6:45 p.m., leaving for night school at 7:15. She returned home again at 10:15. Thus, during four days in the week, she had no leisure time between 7:10 a.m. and 10:15 p.m. In November she dropped out of the class. Is it any wonder that school authorities find the problem of irregular attendance a baffling one?

A Russian girl, living in East 121st Street, worked from 8 to 6 every day in a millinery shop in Fifth Avenue near Thirty-sixth Street. She reached home at 7 o'clock and it was impossible to have dinner and to reach the evening school in 106th Street by 7:30. After being late several times she gave up the effort to attend. The year before she had succeeded in arriving on time by going straight to school from work, and having dinner when she reached home at 10 p.m.

A group of more than a hundred of these evening school pupils who were not yet sixteen years old were interviewed at home by our investigators. Among other questions, they were asked how many hours a day they spent away from home, including time in the workroom, in transit to and from work, and in evening classes. Of 104 questioned on these points, 62 spent an hour or more in transit and only eight spent less than a half hour going to and from work. One hundred were in the workroom nine hours or longer, including the lunch period, and 46 did not reach home until half past six or later in the evening, 34 arriving between 6 and 6:30, and only 24 before 6 o'clock. In work, transit, and evening school four days a week, none of these fourteen- and fifteen-year-old girls spent less than ten hours a day, only seven spent less than twelve hours, while 95 were away from home twelve to fifteen hours of the twenty-four. Two others exceeded even that number. These were all mere children who ought to have been spending several hours in the twenty-four in play and healthful exercise. Yet some of them succeeded in taking a full course in evening school.

Many others, a little older than these children, showed similar powers of endurance. For instance, a packer, sixteen years old, in a department store worked from 8 a.m. to 6 p.m., and on Saturdays until 11 at night, fifty-nine and one-half hours a week, yet she was still in evening high school at the close of the session in May. Furthermore, at Christmas time when the evening schools were closed, she endured the fatigue of working in the store until 11 p.m. every night, thus prolonging the week from fifty-nine and one-half to eighty-two hours. Another, a salesgirl, sixteen years old, employed in a retail store, worked seventy-eight hours in the week before Christmas. On Saturday night of that week she reached home at 12:15 a.m. She was studying bookkeeping, in the hope of getting a better position.

Detailed information of this kind can be secured only through personal interviews with the girls at home. The facts given on the record cards were answers to three questions: What time do you begin work in the morning? How many minutes do you have for lunch at noon? What time do you stop work in the evening? We did not ask for a statement about overtime, since exact information about so complicated a subject would have been difficult to secure in an investigation based, as this one was, on written reports. Nor were the Saturday hours recorded, and therefore the data do not show the length of the working week. The information most significant for the evening schools is the time of stopping work in the evening and the hours of labor on the first four days of the week, when the evening classes are in session.

The hours of work of women in domestic and personal service and in professions were not tabulated. It was evident from the records that the working day in domestic and personal service was so indefinite and so varied that accurate statistics could not be compiled. In the professions the number of women was small and their hours varied too much from group to group to make the combined data significant. The tables, therefore, show the hours of work in the two large occupational groups—manufacturing and mechanical pursuits, and trade and transportation.

Before the facts about hours of labor in manufacturing are accepted as showing present conditions, a word of caution is necessary. In 1912, a year after the investigation was made, a new law went into effect reducing the hours of work of women sixteen years of age and over in factories to fifty-four in a week and nine in a day. The new law, however, permitted under certain conditions a day of ten hours provided the week did not exceed fifty-four hours.* This has resulted in shortening

* The law in effect when the investigation was made limited the working week in factories to sixty and the day to ten hours, with the possibility of extending the day to twelve hours, provided the week did not exceed sixty hours.

the day for women in those trades in which the normal schedule was more than ten hours. Because of this change in the law, an investigation of the hours of labor of evening school pupils made after 1912 would probably give different results from that made in 1911. Doubtless fewer women would be found working ten hours or longer in factories. The law regulating hours of work in stores was changed in the spring of 1914, providing for a nine-hour day and a fifty-four-hour week.* The same law limited the work of children under sixteen to eight hours a day, forty-eight a week, and prohibited their employment at any time except between 8 a.m. and 6 p.m. If these changes in the law be kept in mind, it is safe to regard the records of hours of labor of evening school pupils as representative in the main of conditions in 1913. The daily hours reported by these working girls in 1910–11 are shown in Table 10.

The table shows a marked difference between the two occupational groups—manufacturing and mechanical pursuits, and trade and transportation. In manufacturing, only 15 per cent worked eight hours or less, as compared with 52 per cent in trade and transportation. That the better showing in the latter group, including many occupations

* The law in effect when the investigation was made limited the work of girls between sixteen and twenty-one years of age in mercantile establishments, that is, stores, to sixty hours a week and ten hours a day, except that in order to make one shorter day the hours might be lengthened on five days of the week. The total must not exceed sixty hours. In 1913 the law was extended to protect women of twenty-one years or older. In 1914, the hours were reduced.

TABLE 10.—NORMAL DAILY HOURS OF WORK OF WOMEN ATTENDING PUBLIC EVENING SCHOOLS, EMPLOYED IN MANUFACTURING AND MECHANICAL PURSUITS AND IN TRADE AND TRANSPORTATION[a b]

Daily hours of work[c]	Women working specified hours in			
	Manufacturing and mechanical pursuits		Trade and transportation	
	Number	Per cent	Number	Per cent
Less than 8 hours	129	3.7	1,441	35.6
8 hours	401	11.6	646	16.0
More than 8 hours and less than 9 hours	579	16.7	1,124	27.8
9 hours and less than 10 hours	1,950	56.2	760	18.8
10 hours or more	411	11.8	75	1.8
Total	3,470[b]	100.0	4,046[b]	100.0

[a] Data for women employed in manufacturing and mechanical pursuits appear in detail in Appendix I, Table F, p. 197.

[b] Data relative to hours of work have been tabulated only for women who were employed outside the home at date of investigation. Of the 4,519 who were or had been employed in manufacturing and mechanical pursuits, 190 were unemployed, three worked at home, 658 were in an evening school for which the data as to hours were found to be inaccurate and were not tabulated, and of the 3,668 remaining, 198 did not supply information. Of the 4,505 in trade and transportation, 317 were unemployed, one worked at home, 22 were in an evening school for which the data were not tabulated, and of the 4,165 remaining, 119 did not supply information.

[c] This table shows hours on first five days of the week, not on Saturdays.

besides sales work, is not an indication of short hours in New York stores is shown by a separate tabulation of hours in sales work.* Only 4.5 per cent of the girls in stores worked eight hours or less, while 50 per cent worked between eight and a

* See Appendix I, Table J, p. 201.

half and nine hours a day, 36 per cent between nine and nine and a half, 7.5 per cent working nine and a half hours or longer, and the remaining 2 per cent working more than eight and less than eight and a half hours a day. Of the workers in factories, 68 per cent had a working day of nine hours or more, while only 12 per cent had the much talked of eight-hour day, which has for so long been the goal of the trade unionists. Slightly less than 4 per cent reported a working day of less than eight hours in factories.*

In measuring the length of the day only the actual time of work is counted. The lunch period is deducted. From the hour a girl enters the work place in the morning until she leaves at night is thus a longer time than these data show. The time of beginning and leaving work is shown in Table 11.

To watch the crowds as they walk along the streets in New York every morning on their way to work is to have an interesting object lesson. The earliest of all are the factory girls, as shown by Table 11. Eighty-four out of every 100 of the evening school girls in this group have begun work before 8:30 a.m., and 23 of every hundred must

* Data appear in detail in Appendix I, Table F, p. 197. These figures about hours of work are especially important as the information can not be secured from official reports. The United States census enumerators do not collect facts about hours. The labor department of New York State does not report the hours of work of women separately but includes men in the groups. Moreover, the hours in trade and transportation are not stated in the reports of the labor department for either men or women. The federal bureau of labor now collects and publishes facts about hours but not for all industries nor at regular intervals.

TABLE 11.—HOURS OF BEGINNING AND LEAVING WORK IN MANUFACTURING AND MECHANICAL PURSUITS AND IN TRADE AND TRANSPORTATION, FOR WOMEN ATTENDING PUBLIC EVENING SCHOOLS[a]

Hour of beginning and leaving work[b]	WOMEN BEGINNING OR LEAVING WORK AT SPECIFIED TIME IN			
	Manufacturing and mechanical pursuits		Trade and transportation	
	Number	Per cent	Number	Per cent
Hour of beginning work:				
Before 7 a.m. . . .	3	.1	3	.1
7 a.m. and before 8 a.m. .	814	22.9	115	2.8
8 a.m. and before 8.30 a.m.	2,201	61.8	1,056	25.7
8.30 a.m. and before 9 a.m.	422	11.9	1,442	35.0
9 a.m. or after . .	117	3.3	1,498	36.4
Total reporting . .	3,557[a]	100.0	4,114[a]	100.0
Hour of leaving work:				
Before 5 p.m. . . .	75	2.1	168	4.1
5 p.m. and before 5.30 p.m.	595	16.7	1,075	26.2
5.30 p.m. and before 6 p.m.	1,090	30.5	1,171	28.5
6 p.m.	1,723	48.3	1,512	36.8
After 6 p.m. . . .	86	2.4	179	4.4
Total reporting . .	3,569[a]	100.0	4,105[a]	100.0

[a] Data relative to hours of work have been tabulated only for women who were employed outside the home at date of investigation. Of the 4,519 who were employed in manufacturing and mechanical pursuits, 190 were temporarily unemployed, three worked at home, 658 were in an evening school for which the data as to hours were found to be inaccurate and were not tabulated, and of the 3,668 remaining, 111 did not state hour of beginning work and 99 did not state hour of leaving. Of the 4,505 in trade and transportation, 317 were unemployed, one worked at home, 22 were in an evening school for which the data were not tabulated, and of the 4,165 remaining, 51 did not state hour of beginning work and 60 did not state hour of leaving.

[b] This table shows hour of leaving work on first five days of the week, not on Saturdays.

be in the workroom before eight. Then come the girls who work in offices and stores, of whom 35 per cent must be on duty some time between 8:30 and 9 a.m., while 36 per cent, chiefly clerical workers and stenographers, begin at 9 or a little later.*

In the evening the order of procession is reversed, as the table shows. Of the girls employed in manufacturing, only 19 per cent, as compared with 30 per cent in trade and transportation, stopped work before half past five. Knowing how long a journey in crowded subway or elevated trains many of these girls must take before reaching home, one realizes the significance of the fact that 48 per cent of those employed in factories and 37 per cent in trade and transportation did not leave work until 6 o'clock. A small number in each group worked even later.

Within these large groups, however, are included many different occupations, with widely different schedules of hours. Consider, for example, the main divisions of manufacturing pursuits.† The proportion working nine hours or more daily varied from 43 per cent in millinery to 68 per cent in the manufacture of textiles, 75 per cent in the men's clothing trade, and 82 per cent in the making of women's clothing. Similar differences are found among the different pursuits grouped together as trade and transportation. This means that as the occupational grouping varies from

* For statistics of noon recess, see Appendix I, Table E, p. 196.

† See Appendix I, Table F, p. 197.

school to school and class to class, no two schools and, indeed, no two classes have exactly the same labor conditions with which to reckon. For example, in an evening high school in the Bronx, where 219 women and girls were employed in trade and transportation, as compared with 47 in manufacturing, only 57 of the total of 266 in these two groups, or 21 per cent, worked nine hours or more a day, while in an elementary school in Avenue A, where the numbers in trade and transportation and in manufacturing were almost exactly equal, 185 of a total of 373, or 50 per cent, worked nine hours or longer in a day. On the other hand, it is probable that the girls in the Bronx traveled farther to their work, thus counteracting the benefit of shorter hours at work. In general, however, the problem of the long day's labor is most serious in the schools in which factory girls predominate.

In manufacturing industries, the proportion working eight hours depends in part upon the proportion under sixteen years of age. Because of the eight-hour law for children under sixteen in factories, a group of evening school pupils in a given occupation with a large proportion of children under sixteen among them will probably show a larger proportion working eight hours or less than would be typical of the same occupation, if all its workers had been included in the inquiry. For example, of the girls in evening schools who were employed in flower or feather factories, 36 per cent

Stenographers Practicing Speed

Recreation for Juniors in Evening School

were under sixteen,* as compared with 23 per cent in millinery. The proportion of all the milliners working eight hours or less was 19 per cent, as compared with 37 per cent in flower and feather factories.† The flower trade made a better showing than millinery in the matter of short working hours, because a larger proportion of the flower makers in the evening schools were under sixteen than of the milliners, and not because throughout the flower trade generally a shorter schedule of hours prevails than in millinery shops. Allowance for these differences must be made in studying the statistics. Nevertheless, it should be remembered that the data show the hours of work of girls actually attending evening school, even though in some instances it is probable that other working girls in the same trade, not in the schools, are working longer hours. Naturally, those who are employed shorter hours are better able to attend evening classes.

The hours of work of fourteen- and fifteen-year-old children in evening schools are of special importance. A large part of the interest in industrial education today centers upon the possibility of giving so-called continuation schooling to these young wage-earners after they have left day school. The compulsory education law in New York now requires evening school attendance of all boys

* For age groupings in different occupations, see Appendix I, Table G, p. 198.

† See Appendix I, Table F, p. 197.

under sixteen who go to work before they have graduated from the grammar grades.* While this provision does not apply to girls, its extension to them has not lacked advocates among principals and teachers in the schools, in spite of the fact that other educators and social workers contend that to add evening school work to the day's labor of children of fourteen and fifteen is cruel and unprofitable.

The facts disclosed by the cards of the fourteen- and fifteen-year-old girls in this inquiry will be found to have a bearing not only upon educational problems but upon the enforcement of the labor law. One out of every five girls, 2,632 in all, was not yet sixteen years old. Of these, more than 1,000 were employed in manufacturing and more than 700 in trade and transportation. Table 12 shows the hours of work of the latter group.

Of the 665 girls under sixteen in trade and transportation who reported their hours of work, only 16 per cent worked less than eight hours daily and 16 per cent had an eight-hour day, while 41 per cent worked between eight and nine hours, and 27 per cent worked nine hours or more. Of the 98 stenographers and bookkeepers counted in the

* A recent amendment (New York Laws of 1913) provides that these boys may be required instead to attend part-time classes during the day, in cities or districts where such classes have been established. It provides, also, that girls under sixteen may be required to attend these part-time classes by day. University of the State of New York, Bulletin 535, Jan. 15, 1913, Albany, N. Y. Compulsory Education, p. 3. Experiments in such part-time classes are now being made in New York City.

TABLE 12.—NORMAL DAILY HOURS OF WORK FOR GIRLS UNDER 16 YEARS OF AGE ATTENDING PUBLIC EVENING SCHOOLS, EMPLOYED IN SELECTED OCCUPATIONS IN TRADE AND TRANSPORTATION

Daily hours of work[a]	GIRLS WORKING SPECIFIED HOURS IN					
	Stenography and bookkeeping	Other clerical and office work	Work in stores	Other occupations in trade and transportation	All occupations in trade and transportation	
					Number	Per cent
Less than 8 hours	47	48	8	1	104	15.6
8 hours	24	70	5	9	108	16.2
More than 8 hours and less than 9 hours	17	109	128	21	275	41.4
9 hours and less than 10 hours	9	64	69	28	170	25.6
10 hours or more	1	2	3	2	8	1.2
Total	98	293	213	61	665[b]	100.0

[a] This table shows hours on first five days of the week, not on Saturdays.

[b] Of the 740 girls under sixteen years of age who were employed in trade and transportation, 10 were in an evening school for which data as to hours were found to be inaccurate and were not tabulated, 44 were unemployed at the date of the investigation, and 21 did not supply information.

group, 71 worked eight hours or less, while of the 293 other clerical workers, 175, or three-fifths, worked more than eight hours. Among the girls employed in stores, including cash girls, the largest group, 128 worked between eight and nine hours. Evidently the hours in these occupations are not short, even for girls under sixteen. The state law, indeed, at the time of the investigation permitted the employment of these children in mercantile establishments nine hours a day and prohibited their work before 8 a.m. and after 7 p.m.*

In manufacturing establishments the law provides that no child between the ages of fourteen and sixteen years shall be employed more than eight hours in any one day, or forty-eight in a week. Furthermore, the eight hours daily must be between 8 in the morning and 5 at night. Table 13 shows the hours of work of evening school girls under sixteen in factories.

Of 898 girls under sixteen who were at work in factories at the date of the investigation and who recorded hours of labor, 592, or 66 per cent, were working longer than the law permitted. The violations shown in the table were not mere technical slips; they were serious and flagrant. Of the 592 girls working longer than eight hours, 393 were working nine hours or more, as though the

* In 1914, the mercantile law was brought into conformity with the factory law, in the regulation of the hours of children's work, restricting them to eight daily and forty-eight weekly, except that they may work until 6 p.m. in stores, offices, and so forth, instead of stopping at 5 o'clock, as in factories.

TABLE 13.—NORMAL DAILY HOURS OF WORK OF GIRLS UNDER 16 YEARS OF AGE ATTENDING PUBLIC EVENING SCHOOLS, EMPLOYED IN SELECTED OCCUPATIONS IN MANUFACTURING AND MECHANICAL PURSUITS

Daily hours of work [a]	GIRLS WORKING SPECIFIED HOURS IN							
	Artificial flower and feather making	Making of women's clothing	Millinery	Work on printing and paper goods	Work on textiles	Other manufacturing and mechanical pursuits	All manufacturing and mechanical pursuits	
							Number	Per cent
Less than 8 hours	16	7	6	1	2	11	43	4.8
8 hours	28	48	8	42	36	101	263	29.3
More than 8 hours and less than 9 hours	29	58	12	26	14	60	199	22.2
9 hours and less than 10 hours	17	147	25	33	15	101	338	37.6
10 hours or more	1	25	1	2	11	15	55	6.1
Total	91	285	52	104	78	288	898 [b]	100.0

[a] This table shows hours on first five days of the week, not on Saturdays.

[b] Of the total 1,044 under sixteen years of age who were employed in manufacturing, 58 were at evening school for which data as to hours were found to be inaccurate and were not tabulated, 59 were unemployed at the date of the investigation, and 29 did not supply information.

eight-hour law, whose enactment was brought about through the efforts of so many persons interested in the welfare of children, had never been placed on the statute books. Six per cent of these children were working ten hours or longer. In a number of instances two or three provisions of the law were violated in a single position, and thus the number of violations is larger than the number of workers experiencing them. Counting each violation as one, as it would be counted in a court of law, the record cards revealed 1,201 violations of the law, of which the offense "more than eight hours daily" numbered 592; "before 8 a.m.," 96; and "after 5 p.m.," 513.

This is serious. The New York child labor law is regarded as a model—on paper. But the community's responsibility does not end when the legislature passes a model law. The task of enforcement demands sustained public interest and effective machinery to make that interest felt. The statements of these girls in evening schools indicated very imperfect enforcement of the law designed to protect them against overwork in factories.

To test the accuracy of the statements made on the record cards, 108, nearly one-fifth, of the girls who reported illegal hours were visited at home. They were questioned about their employment and all its conditions, and no reference was made by the visitor to the eight-hour law. In this way the facts about hours were corroborated. The statements had shown that eight of these 108 were employed before 8 a.m., 77 after 5 p.m., 90 more than eight hours daily, and 79 more than forty-eight hours weekly; 254 distinct violations in the group of 108 girls. Only 16 of these girls made statements to the visitor which failed to sustain the earlier report of violations, and of these, only six revised the report of hours, five were found to be employed in establishments not coming within the scope of the eight-hour law, and the five others were sixteen years old and had stated their age incorrectly on the cards. Of the 108 interviewed, not only did 92 repeat the facts previously recorded, but 33 reported 107 other violations of this same law in other jobs which they had held. In 10 cases the girls had begun work without employment certificates, an additional type of violation not shown on the record card.

These violations were not limited to any one trade nor to any one type of evening school. While the visits were confined to girls living in Manhattan, these included pupils in all of the evening high schools for girls in that borough, and in 14 evening elementary schools.* Table 13 shows long hours for children in the making of artificial flowers and feathers, women's clothing, millinery, printing and paper goods, and textiles. The children who were interviewed in order to verify their reports of illegal hours were at work in laundries, paper box factories, bookbinderies, dressmaking shops, and more than two dozen other trades.

* Numbers 4, 13, 14, 19, 23, 29, 38, 45, 59, 71, 72, 92, 96, and 177.

In exempting girls from required legal attendance at evening school, the danger of overtaxing their strength has been recognized.* The age limit of admittance has indeed been gradually raised during the years since the evening schools were first organized. The board of education in its report for 1865 recommended that no boy under fourteen and no girl under twelve be admitted to evening school. The presence of children kept young men and women away, it contended. At that time children were admitted without regard to age. "The result is," said the report, "that we have every winter from five to six thousand children under twelve years of age in our evening schools."† Many of these were not more than eight years old. A large proportion were at work in stores or factories, and so overtaxed were they by the day's labor that they fell asleep in the class rooms. In 1866 children under twelve were excluded.

Since those days the child labor law has put a stop to the employment of very young children in industry, and the compulsory education law keeps

* Instances were discovered by our visitors in which the parents of girls under sixteen had, unfortunately, been given the impression that girls also are compelled to attend evening school. For example, the following postal card had been sent out by the schools:

"To Parents: Under the provisions of the Compulsory Education Law, all children between fourteen and sixteen who leave day school to go to work must attend evening school.

"Parents are requested to send word immediately to the principal of the day school in which evening school the child has registered." (Signed by a district superintendent.) (Also printed in Yiddish on lower half of card.) The wording, of course, should have been "all boys" instead of "all children."

† Board of Education, New York City. Report of 1865; Appendix. Report of City Superintendent of Schools, p. 55.

them in day school until they are fourteen, so that the sleepy little eight-year-olds no longer trouble evening school teachers. But the fourteen-year-old wage-earning boy who has not graduated still causes trouble both when he fails to obey the law compelling him to continue to go to night school, and when he fulfils the arduous requirement. In one case he must be kept attending, and in the other he must be kept awake. Each annual report refers with slight verbal changes to "the difficulties attendant upon the enforcement of a law approved neither by popular sentiment nor by the wisest educational considerations."* A forward step was taken when in 1913 the law already mentioned was passed, giving power to boards of education in the cities and districts of the state to require children under sixteen who are at work to attend part-time classes between the hours of 8 a.m. and 5 p.m. Before this law can bring relief to children under sixteen in evening schools in New York City, however, part-time classes by day must be established there. This will bring our educational policy more closely in accord with the real intent of the laws restricting the work of children to hours between 8 in the morning and 5 at night in factories.

Had it been possible to discover the amount of overtime which may have been added to the normal day's work of all girls over sixteen, doubt-

* Superintendent of Schools, New York City. Fourteenth Annual Report, 1911–12. Report on Evening Schools for the Year Ending July 31, 1912, p. 72.

less, many instances of exhaustingly long hours would have been brought to light. It is a common experience in working girls' clubs, as well as in public evening classes, to find the program upset because some of the members are "working late."* Study of state labor department reports shows that prosecutions for illegally long hours have been few in number, indicating lax enforcement. Those who watch the progress of labor bills in the legislature know that any attempt to strengthen the law meets with vigorous opposition from employers. Yet protection of women and young girls against overwork is one of the most important tasks before the community. Until these laws are strengthened and enforced, wage-earning girls can not take full advantage of the education which the community endeavors to give them in evening classes.

* In his report of 1912–13, Dr. Albert Shiels, district superintendent in charge of evening schools in New York City, outlined the result of inquiries which he had caused to be made regarding reasons for irregular attendance. In seven of the evening high schools, 1,362 pupils reported reasons for leaving before the close of the session, and of these, 542, or nearly 40 per cent, said that "night work including overtime," was responsible. In evening trade schools the same reason was the most prominent, being given by 299 of 1,006; in evening elementary schools, in classes for foreigners, cards sent to 200 who had left brought replies from 159, of whom 105 said that they were working overtime. A group of pupils whose combined absences during the term had amounted to 865 evenings, were questioned as to the reasons, and overtime work was assigned as the cause of absence on 324 of these 865 evenings.—Superintendent of Schools, New York City. Fifteenth Annual Report, 1912–13. Report on Evening Schools for the Year Ending July 31, 1913, pp. 67–71.

CHAPTER IV

SCHOOLING OF WAGE-EARNING GIRLS

DISCUSSION of industrial education usually centers about the class rooms of today and the children who are now in school. It emphasizes the need for giving these children adequate preparation for the demands which will probably be made upon them in their future careers as breadwinners. New light is thrown on the subject when this process of inquiry is reversed. Instead of theorizing about the probable future of the present school children, it is possible to discover the past school careers of present wage-earners. By this method we may gradually learn, among other things, whether the length of the schooling and the age when wage-earning began seem to have any bearing on the choice of an occupation. To gather this kind of information, however, is not easy, since it is not to be found in any documents but must be secured from the wage-earners themselves. The fact that so large a group of working girls answered questions about their previous schooling is one of the unique features of this study of evening school pupils.

The questions on this subject were simple and detailed:

How old were you when you began school?
Did you graduate from elementary school?
What grade were you in when you left?
How old were you when you left?
In what school did you attend first grade? (This question was repeated for every grade from the first to the eighth.)
What day high schools have you attended?
How many years did you attend?
How old were you when you left?

The most important material to be derived from the answers included the number of years in school; the types of schools attended and their location, whether in New York or in other parts of this country, or in foreign lands; the grade reached; and the age at leaving. Such facts show not only the educational foundation on which the evening schools must build, but they reveal certain conditions to be reckoned with in the development of a scheme of industrial training.

In discussing vocational education the tendency seems to be to regard the population as stationary for all time; to assume that the wage-earners of today were school children in this community a few years ago, and that the school children of today will be working in the factories, stores, and offices of this city a few years from now.* Yet everyone knows how comparatively rare a specimen is the

* For significant facts on this subject see Ayres, Leonard P.: Some Conditions Affecting Problems of Industrial Education in 78 American School Systems. Pamphlet published by Division of Education, Russell Sage Foundation, No. E 135, February, 1914.

native New Yorker who still lives in the city of his birth, and how many of his fellow-citizens have come from the four quarters of the globe. Among the wage-earning women in New York City, in 1900, 55 per cent were born in the United States, and scarcely more than one in six was native born of native parentage.* These figures do not show how many of those who are counted as native born were actually born in New York City, and how many in other sections of the United States. Of course some of those who were born in foreign lands came to New York as children and went to New York schools. Nevertheless, that many receive at least a part of their schooling elsewhere is shown in the records of evening school pupils. It should be remembered that as pupils in classes in English for foreigners were not as a rule included in the inquiry, the group investigated contains a larger proportion of native born than is found among all wage-earning women throughout the city; 68 per cent in our records† as compared with 55 per cent in the census statistics. Nevertheless, even in the selected group investigated by us the diversity of schools attended is noteworthy, as Table 14 shows.

According to this table, 71 per cent of the girls

* Twelfth United States Census, 1900. Special Reports, Occupations, p. 638. Of 367,437 wage-earning women, 56,027 were native born of native parents, 128,830 were native born of foreign parents, and 16,155 were colored (chiefly native born), making, roughly, a total of 200,000 native born. Of the girls employed in manufacturing, 57.9 per cent were native born (76,694 of 132,535).

† See Table 2, p. 21.

TABLE 14.—DAY SCHOOLS PREVIOUSLY ATTENDED AT ANY TIME BY WOMEN ATTENDING PUBLIC EVENING SCHOOLS, BY PRINCIPAL OCCUPATIONAL GROUPS

Schools previously attended	WOMEN EMPLOYED IN					All women
	Manufacturing and mechanical pursuits	Trade and transportation	Domestic and personal service	Professional service	No gainful occupation[a]	
Women reporting[b]	3,421	4,399	471	193	3,261	11,745[c]
Number who attended						
New York City public schools	2,184	3,664	85	153	2,271	8,357
New York City parochial and private schools	630	817	38	40	568	2,093
Other schools in the United States outside New York City	180	351	115	26	358	1,030
Schools in foreign countries	845	245	206	11	460	1,767
No day school	34	4	45	..	12	95
Per cent who attended						
New York City public schools	63.8	83.3	18.0	79.3	69.6	71.2
New York City parochial and private schools	18.4	18.6	8.1	20.7	17.4	17.8
Other schools in the United States outside New York City	5.3	8.0	24.4	13.5	11.0	8.8
Schools in foreign countries	24.7	5.6	43.7	5.7	14.1	15.0
No day school	1.0	.1	9.6	....	.4	.8

[a] For further explanation, see footnote, p. 36.

[b] As some women had attended schools of two or more types, the sum of the items in each column exceeds the total appearing at the head of the column.

[c] Of the 13,141 women included in the study, 896 were in evening schools for which data as to all day schools attended at any time were incomplete and were not tabulated. Of the 12,245 remaining, 500 did not supply information.

investigated had at some time attended public schools in New York City, and 18 per cent, private or parochial schools there, while 8.8 per cent had attended schools in other communities of the United States, and 15 per cent, schools in foreign lands. These groups are not mutually exclusive. A girl may have gone to school in Russia, Germany, or Italy, then in a small town in Connecticut, and finally she may have been found in a class room on the lower East Side of New York. She will be counted in each of the groups of schools reported. One girl, born in South Africa of German parentage, went to school first in England, then in South Africa, again in England, and finally in New York.

The differences between the different occupational groups in Table 14 indicate what is perhaps the most valuable point brought out by this study. In trade and transportation and in professional service the proportion who have attended New York public schools is much larger than in manufacturing,—83 per cent in trade and transportation, 79 per cent in professional service, and 64 per cent in manufacturing. If we make allowance for the fact that the proportion of native born in this group of factory workers is larger than in the same occupational group in the general population, it seems probable that not more than 60 per cent of the wage-earning girls in the factories of the city have ever attended a public school in New York. The bearing of this on plans to train children in this city for the trades which they are expected to enter later is obviously important. Evidently the day schools can not handle alone the problem of vocational training. For a large proportion of our wage-earners the evening schools represent the only opportunity to come under the influence of our system of public education, whether the aim be industrial education or academic instruction. Table 15 gives added emphasis to the facts already cited by showing the location of the last day school attended by these evening school pupils.

A New York public school was named as the last day school attended by 67 per cent of the group, and a parochial or private school in New York by 12 per cent. Again the differences between different occupational groups are marked. In manufacturing, 24 per cent had had their last schooling in a foreign country and 57 per cent in New York public schools, as compared with 81 per cent in New York public schools in the group employed in trade and transportation. The figures in this table take no account of special courses attended later, as in business schools, art classes, or normal schools. The aim was to show rather where the basic education was secured before any specialized training was begun.

That the school histories of these girls were varied as their families may have journeyed from one community to another has already been indicated. The proportion who received their entire schooling in New York public schools is shown in Table 16.

TABLE 15.—LAST DAY SCHOOL ATTENDED BY WOMEN ATTENDING PUBLIC EVENING SCHOOLS, BY PRINCIPAL OCCUPATIONAL GROUPS[a]

Last day school attended	Women employed in					All women
	Manufacturing and mechanical pursuits	Trade and transportation	Domestic and personal service	Professional service	No gainful occupation[b]	
Number who attended						
New York City public school	2,212	3,548	77	149	2,188	8,174
New York City parochial or private school	476	525	34	17	418	1,470
Elementary school in the United States outside New York City	85	99	95	2	199	480
High school in the United States outside New York City	18	101	15	15	67	216
School in a foreign country	937	130	208	9	394	1,678
No day school	188	5	47	..	18	258
Total	3,916	4,408	476	192	3,284	12,276[c]
Per cent who attended						
New York City public school	56.5	80.5	16.2	77.6	66.7	66.5
New York City parochial or private school	12.1	11.9	7.1	8.9	12.7	12.0
Elementary school in the United States outside New York City	2.2	2.2	19.9	1.0	6.1	3.9
High school in the United States outside New York City	.5	2.3	3.2	7.8	2.0	1.8
School in a foreign country	23.9	3.0	43.7	4.7	12.0	13.7
No day school	4.8	.1	9.9	....	.5	2.1
Total	100.0	100.0	100.0	100.0	100.0	100.0

[a] Data, in part, appear in more detail in Appendix I, Table J, p. 201. [b] For further explanation, see footnote, p. 36. [c] Of the 13,141 women included in the study, 865 did not supply information.

TABLE 16.—PROPORTION OF WOMEN ATTENDING PUBLIC EVENING SCHOOLS, WHOSE ONLY PREVIOUS DAY SCHOOL ATTENDANCE WAS IN NEW YORK PUBLIC SCHOOLS, BY PRINCIPAL OCCUPATIONAL GROUPS

Principal occupational group	WOMEN WHO HAD ATTENDED			All women
	New York public schools only	Other schools[a]	No school	
Manufacturing and mechanical pursuits				
Number	1,562	1,825	34	3,421
Per cent	45.7	53.3	1.0	100.0
Trade and transportation				
Number	2,948	1,447	4	4,399
Per cent	67.0	32.9	.1	100.0
Domestic and personal service				
Number	59	367	45	471
Per cent	12.5	77.9	9.6	100.0
Professional service				
Number	109	84	..	193
Per cent	56.5	43.5	..	100.0
No gainful occupation[b]				
Number	1,842	1,407	12	3,261
Per cent	56.5	43.1	.4	100.0
Total				
Number	6,520	5,130	95	11,745[c]
Per cent	55.5	43.7	.8	100.0

[a] Women who had attended New York public day schools and also some other school or schools, are included in this column.

[b] For further explanation, see footnote, p. 36.

[c] Of the 13,141 women included in the study, 896 were in evening schools for which data as to all day schools attended at any time were incomplete and were not tabulated. Of the 12,245 remaining, 500 did not supply information.

The New York public school system was wholly responsible for the training of 6,520, or 56 per cent, of the entire group investigated. In manufacturing, the proportion educated in New York public schools was only 46 per cent, and in trade and transportation it was 67 per cent.

Because of the diversity of schools attended, throughout this country and in others, it would be unwise to attempt a tabulation of grades reached which would include the whole group investigated. The grading is not uniform even in different cities of the United States, and for other countries no common basis of instruction could be found. Concerning those whose last schooling was in New York public schools, however, some interesting statistics are available.

One of the most baffling problems of industrial training is the fact that many children leave the elementary grades as soon as the law permits them to go to work. The schools are expected to accomplish so large a task as "preparation for life" in so brief a period as lies between babyhood and the fourteenth birthday. The New York state labor law prohibits the employment of children under fourteen, and requires that those who go to work between the ages of fourteen and sixteen must be provided with employment certificates. To secure an employment certificate, the child must have accomplished satisfactorily a specified amount of schooling. Until 1913 it was necessary to have reached the 5B grade, the fifth year of schooling, but an amendment to the law in that year required the completion of the work of the first six years of a public elementary school or its equivalent.*

In the sixth grade of New York public schools the children are studying percentage and its applications, the geography of Europe, American history since the war of 1812, English, music, drawing, and if they are girls, sewing. Gymnastic exercises and hygiene are also part of the curriculum. Two more years lie between them and graduation, and in that time they would be initiated further into the mysteries of all these studies. In mathematics, for example, the sixth grade children have learned nothing of simple interest, ratio and proportion, equations, and square root, which are taught in the seventh and eighth grades. In history the sixth grade child has not extended his knowledge beyond the United States. The study of European history begins in the seventh grade.†

Of course, these statements taken from the printed outline of the prescribed course of study can not be accepted literally as an inventory of the facts collected in the brain of the sixth grade boy or girl. The content of a simple lesson in English composition may be rich in historical facts, or

* In New York the grades are numbered consecutively from one to eight, beginning with the lowest. Each grade is divided into two parts, designated as A and B, the two together covering the school year. A normal pupil is expected to complete one grade in a year, so that if he begins at the age of six he may accomplish his eight grades and graduate at fourteen.

† Course of Study for the Elementary Schools of the City of New York, 1911. Department of Education.

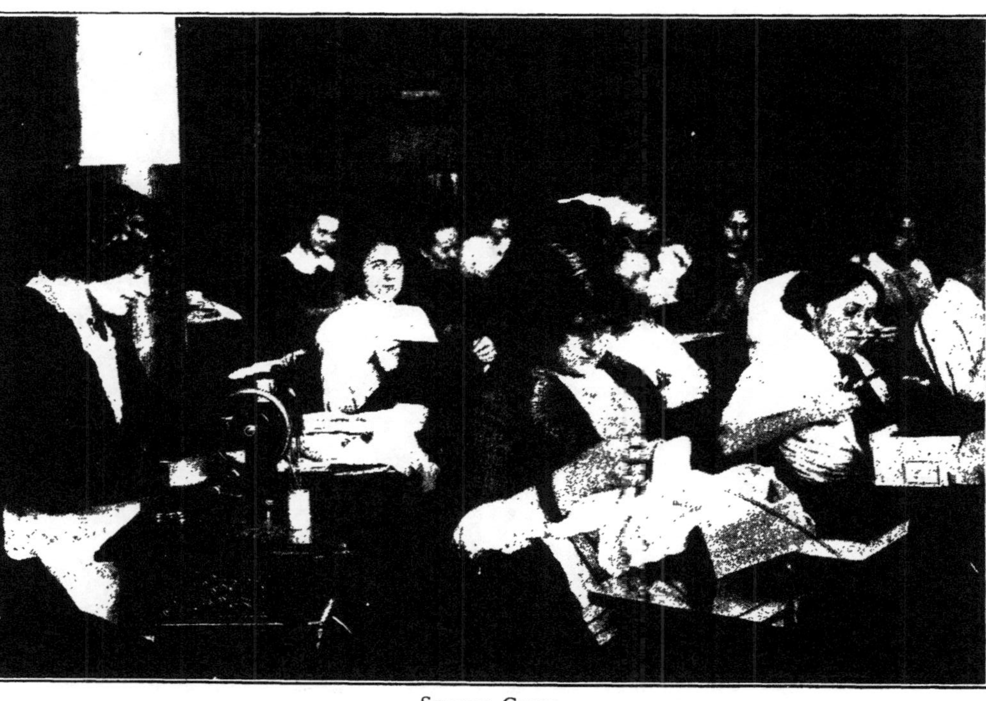

Sewing Class
Handicapped by small desks

nature study, or ethical principles, and the curriculum can never be more than a series of guide posts. Nevertheless, it is obvious that not a very large part of the road to knowledge can be traversed between the sixth and the fourteenth years of childhood, even if eight grades be completed in that time. Table 17 shows the grade reached by 7,854 girls who last attended New York City public schools and who have since returned to evening classes.

The table shows the grade reached in school by women now at work in the specified occupational groups, and reveals great differences in amount of previous schooling between workers in the different occupations represented. In professional service 72 per cent were high school graduates; in manufacturing and mechanical pursuits, a small fraction of 1 per cent (.2 per cent). Among the factory girls one-third left school when in the sixth grade or below, and nearly three-fifths before reaching the eighth grade. In trade and transportation a large proportion, 76 per cent, finished the elementary grades and 28 per cent went to high school, only 2.1 per cent graduating, however. In the ranks of women at work in domestic and personal service only 23 per cent had graduated from elementary school, and only 33 per cent had ever gone beyond the seventh grade. Apparently the child who leaves elementary school before graduating is most likely to earn her living in factory work or in domestic or personal service, while if she graduates she will have more chance of

TABLE 17.—GRADE AT LEAVING SCHOOL FOR WOMEN ATTENDING PUBLIC EVENING SCHOOLS, WHO LAST ATTENDED DAY SCHOOL IN A NEW YORK PUBLIC SCHOOL, BY PRINCIPAL OCCUPATIONAL GROUPS

Grade at leaving school	Women employed in: Manufacturing and mechanical pursuits	Trade and transportation	Domestic and personal service	Professional service	No gainful occupation[a]	All women
Number who left when						
In first grade . .	4	..	..	..	..	4
In second grade .	9	1	3	..	4	17
In third grade . .	10	1	2	..	8	21
In fourth grade .	51	11	5	..	33	100
In fifth grade . .	196	44	13	..	96	349
In sixth grade . .	397	181	9	..	185	772
In seventh grade .	528	353	15	3	343	1,242
In eighth grade .	196	255	7	4	189	651
Elem. sch. graduate	499	1,683	11	20	682	2,895
High school non-graduate . .	133	901	4	14	524	1,576
High school graduate	4	74	1	107	41	227
Total . . .	2,027	3,504	70	148	2,105	7,854[b]
Per cent who left when						
In first grade . .	.2	....[c]	....	....	....	.1
In second grade .	.4	....[c]	4.3	....	.2	.2
In third grade . .	.5	....	2.9	....	.4	.3
In fourth grade .	2.5	.3	7.1	....	1.6	1.3
In fifth grade . .	9.7	1.3	18.6	....	4.6	4.4
In sixth grade . .	19.6	5.2	12.9	....	8.8	9.8
In seventh grade .	26.0	10.1	21.4	2.0	16.3	15.8
In eighth grade .	9.7	7.3	10.0	2.7	9.0	8.3
Elem. sch. graduate	24.6	48.0	15.7	13.5	32.3	36.8
High school non-graduate . .	6.6	25.7	5.7	9.5	24.9	20.1
High school graduate	.2	2.1	1.4	72.3	1.9	2.9
Total . . .	100.0	100.0	100.0	100.0	100.0	100.0

[a] For further explanation, see footnote, p. 36.

[b] Of the 8,174 who last attended day school in a New York public school (see Table 15), 155 were in two evening schools which supplied no further information as to schooling, and of the 8,019 remaining, 165 did not state grade at leaving. For years in high school, see Appendix I, Table I, p. 200. [c] Less than .05 per cent.

employment in trade and transportation, and if she finishes high school she is on the road to some form of professional work. Or again, interpreting the figures from another point of view, we seem justified in saying that it is only in the first seven grades that the schools under present conditions are in contact with the majority of the future employes in factory industries. Nevertheless, in the different branches of manufacturing the schooling of employes varies widely, as Table 18 shows.

Of the milliners, 41 per cent left school before reaching the eighth grade; in dressmaking, 55 per cent; and in the artificial flower and feather trade and in bookbinding, 49 per cent, as compared with 79 per cent in paper box making. The elementary school graduates, including those who went to high school, numbered 49 per cent in millinery, 39 per cent in dressmaking, 38 per cent in flower and feather making, 29 per cent in bookbinding, and only 16 per cent in paper box making.

These figures tempt one to analyze available data showing comparative wages paid in these different trades, as a basis for estimating the comparative amount of skill required. In 1905, census enumerators copied payrolls showing actual earnings received by workers in a representative week of the year in a large number of manufacturing establishments. The facts presented for women workers in New York State* show that the

* United States Census, Bulletin 93, Earnings of Wage-Earners, Manufactures, pp. 98 and 150. 1905.

TABLE 18.—GRADE AT LEAVING SCHOOL FOR WOMEN ATTENDING PUBLIC EVENING SCHOOLS, WHO LAST ATTENDED DAY SCHOOL IN A NEW YORK PUBLIC SCHOOL, EMPLOYED IN FIVE SELECTED MANUFACTURING PURSUITS[a b]

Grade at leaving school	WOMEN[a] EMPLOYED IN				
	Millinery	Dressmaking	Artificial flower and feather making	Bookbinding	Paper box making
Number who left when					
In first grade	..	..	..	..	..
In second grade	..	3	..	..	..
In third grade	1	1	..	1	..
In fourth grade	2	4	4	2	2
In fifth grade	6	22	18	2	12
In sixth grade	19	30	31	14	22
In seventh grade	32	62	43	21	16
In eighth grade	14	13	26	18	3
Elem. sch. graduate	48	65	57	18	9
High school non-graduate	21	19	16	6	1
High school graduate	2	..	..	..	..
Total	145	219	195	82	65
Per cent who left when					
In first grade	..	..	..	..	..
In second grade	..	1	..	..	..
In third grade	1	..	..	1	..
In fourth grade	1	2	2	2	3
In fifth grade	4	10	9	2	18
In sixth grade	13	14	16	18	33
In seventh grade	22	28	22	26	25
In eighth grade	10	6	13	22	5
Elem. sch. graduate	33	30	30	22	14
High school non-graduate	15	9	8	7	2
High school graduate	1	..	..	..	..
Total	100	100	100	100	100

[a] Data appear in detail in Appendix I, Table K, p. 207.

[b] Information was not supplied by 9 of the 154 milliners, 10 of the 229 dressmakers, 23 of the 218 flower and feather makers, 3 of the 85 bookbinders, and 4 of the 69 paper box makers, who last attended day school in a New York public school.

average weekly earnings of milliners were $7.63; makers of women's clothing, $7.68; artificial flower and feather makers, $6.20;* bookbinders, $6.13; paper box makers, $5.65; and of women in all manufacturing pursuits grouped together, $6.54.

Only detailed study of these trades would enable us safely to conclude that these averages indicate the comparative degree of skill required in these trades, and it would be another long step in the argument to say that the higher the grade reached in school, the better the chance to enter a skilled occupation. It may be only a coincidence that in paper box making the average wage is lower than in any other of these five trades, while among paper box makers in evening schools the general level of education as measured by the proportion of pupils who have never passed beyond the seventh grade is also the lowest. Nevertheless, the coincidence suggests an interesting line of inquiry to determine the comparative demand in different vocations for the kind of training now offered by the schools.

In the records of progress made in day school, it is possible to discover further clues as to an apparent connection between the adaptability of a pupil to the present school training and the later choice of an occupation. To avoid the danger of comparing groups trained in different types of schools and different communities, the group dis-

* Given for the whole United States, but as three-fourths of the industry is in New York City, the figures are indicative of wage rates there.

cussed will be limited to those who received their entire schooling in New York public schools. It will be recalled that this group numbered 6,520, or 56 per cent of the number investigated.* As already outlined, the pupil who makes normal progress in a New York public school is expected to complete one grade in a year. By comparing the number of years in the school life with the grade reached we may, therefore, measure the rate of progress. A pupil who has attended school six years may be rated as normal if she has reached grade 6B or 7A, slow if in a lower grade, and rapid if she has advanced further. Table 19 shows the progress made in day school by women in different occupational groups.

Of the whole group, 34 per cent showed normal progress, 22 per cent rapid, and 44 per cent retarded progress. The proportion of the retarded was highest in domestic and personal service, 74 per cent; with manufacturing second, 59 per cent; and women without any occupation third, 46 per cent. Women in professional service showed the smallest proportion retarded, and the largest proportion whose progress had been rapid. Thus it appears to be the girls whose present occupations require pre-eminently the use of the hands who during their school days were least able to keep pace with the curriculum. "There was no larnin' in her," said one mother when asked why her daughter left school.

* See Table 16, p. 90.

TABLE 19.—PROGRESS MADE IN ELEMENTARY SCHOOL BY WOMEN ATTENDING PUBLIC EVENING SCHOOLS, WHO HAD ATTENDED NEW YORK PUBLIC SCHOOLS ONLY, BY PRINCIPAL OCCUPATIONAL GROUPS

Principal occupational group	Women in each specified occupational group whose progress had been			All women
	Rapid	Normal	Retarded	
Manufacturing and mechanical pursuits				
Number	206	369	824	1,399
Per cent	14.7	26.4	58.9	100.0
Trade and transportation				
Number	703	980	929	2,612
Per cent	26.9	37.5	35.6	100.0
Domestic and personal service				
Number	6	7	36	49
Per cent	12.2	14.3	73.5	100.0
Professional service				
Number	28	35	30	93
Per cent	30.1	37.6	32.3	100.0
No gainful occupation [a]				
Number	307	541	710	1,558
Per cent	19.7	34.7	45.6	100.0
Total				
Number	1,250	1,932	2,529	5,711 [b]
Per cent	21.9	33.8	44.3	100.0

[a] For further explanation, see footnote, p. 36.

[b] Of the 6,520 whose entire elementary schooling was in the New York public schools, 809 did not supply information.

The learned in the population have, as a rule, had long school careers lasting, perhaps, from kindergarten at the age of five or six until graduation from college at twenty-one or twenty-two. Following the college course comes frequently some form of professional training. The educational process, aside from professional courses, covers fifteen or sixteen years. For those who have had such opportunities it is exceedingly difficult to imagine how different would have been their development in character, mentality, and physical vitality, had their school life been cut short after eight years instead of sixteen. For the majority of wage-earning girls in New York, schooling is a comparatively brief experience. Table 20 gives the facts for the girls investigated in evening school. The table includes all the girls who gave information on this point and not only those who had attended New York schools.

The proportion who had had nine years or more of schooling was 33 per cent for the whole group, but only 23 per cent for the group in manufacturing and 24 per cent for those in domestic and personal service, as compared with 38 per cent in trade and transportation and 81 per cent in the professions. That many stay in the schools as long as seven or eight years is doubtless due, in New York at least, to the child labor law forbidding the employment of children under fourteen. In studying the records showing the age at leaving school, therefore, the significant year to watch is the fifteenth, the earliest moment when a child may go to work. The data obtained appear in Table 21.

The table includes, of course, older women who went to work before the present law was in force, and others who went to school in foreign lands or in districts of this country where the child labor

TABLE 20.—YEARS OF ATTENDANCE AT DAY SCHOOL FOR WOMEN ATTENDING PUBLIC EVENING SCHOOLS, BY PRINCIPAL OCCUPATIONAL GROUPS

Years of attendance	WOMEN EMPLOYED IN					All women
	Manufacturing and mechanical pursuits	Trade and transportation	Domestic and personal service	Professional service	No gainful occupation[a]	
Number who attended						
Less than 5 years	212	23	77	..	81	393
5 years and less than 6 years	135	54	22	1	87	299
6 years and less than 7 years	270	218	37	4	200	729
7 years and less than 8 years	585	772	51	5	511	1,924
8 years and less than 9 years	958	1,342	86	21	917	3,324
9 years and less than 10 years	446	864	40	21	495	1,866
10 years or more	210	604	58	107	510	1,489
Number who never attended day school	34	4	45	..	12	95
Total	2,850	3,881	416	159	2,813	10,119[b]
Per cent who attended						
Less than 5 years	7.4	.6	18.5	....	2.9	3.9
5 years and less than 6 years	4.7	1.4	5.3	.6	3.1	3.0
6 years and less than 7 years	9.5	5.6	8.9	2.5	7.1	7.2
7 years and less than 8 years	20.5	19.9	12.3	3.1	18.2	19.0
8 years and less than 9 years	33.7	34.5	20.7	13.2	32.6	32.9
9 years and less than 10 years	15.6	22.3	9.6	13.2	17.6	18.4
10 years or more	7.4	15.6	13.9	67.4	18.1	14.7
Per cent who never attended day school	1.2	.1	10.8	....	.4	.9
Total	100.0	100.0	100.0	100.0	100.0	100.0

[a] For further explanation, see footnote, p. 36.

[b] Of the 13,141 women included in the study, 896 were in evening schools for which this information was incomplete and was not tabulated. Of the 12,245 remaining, 2,126 did not supply information.

TABLE 21.—AGE AT LEAVING DAY SCHOOL OF WOMEN ATTENDING PUBLIC EVENING SCHOOLS, BY PRINCIPAL OCCUPATIONAL GROUPS

Age at leaving day school	WOMEN EMPLOYED IN					All women
	Manufacturing and mechanical pursuits	Trade and transportation	Domestic and personal service	Professional service	No gainful occupation[a]	
Number who left when						
Less than 14 years	517	410	124	5	455	1,511
14 years and less than 15 years	1,498	1,564	115	15	1,086	4,278
15 years and less than 16 years	708	1,217	68	24	669	2,686
16 years and less than 17 years	244	578	46	21	431	1,320
17 years and less than 18 years	52	184	18	26	167	447
18 years or more	36	89	15	75	124	339
Number who never attended day school	34	4	45	..	12	95
Total	3,089	4,046	431	166	2,944	10,676[b]
Per cent who left when						
Less than 14 years	16.7	10.1	28.7	3.0	15.5	14.1
14 years and less than 15 years	48.5	38.7	26.7	9.0	36.9	40.1
15 years and less than 16 years	22.9	30.1	15.8	14.5	22.7	25.1
16 years and less than 17 years	7.9	14.3	10.7	12.7	14.6	12.4
17 years and less than 18 years	1.7	4.5	4.2	15.7	5.7	4.2
18 years or more	1.2	2.2	3.5	45.1	4.2	3.2
Per cent who never attended day school	1.1	.1	10.4	....	.4	.9
Total	100.0	100.0	100.0	100.0	100.0	100.0

[a] For further explanation, see page 36.

[b] Of the 13,141 women included in the study, 896 were in evening schools for which this information was incomplete and was not tabulated. Of the 12,245 remaining, 1,569 did not state age at leaving day school.

and compulsory education laws are not the same as in New York. Not all, therefore, were restrained by law from going to work before they were fourteen. Of all the girls considered, more than half, 54 per cent, had left at the age of fourteen or younger, and only 20 per cent stayed until they were sixteen or older. The best showing is made by the professional workers, with 45 per cent having attended school till they were eighteen or older, as compared with 1.2 per cent in manufacturing and 2.2 per cent in trade and transportation. Of the girls in manufacturing, 65 per cent left at the age of fourteen or younger, as compared with 49 per cent in trade and transportation. That many in both these groups stayed until they were fifteen was undoubtedly due in part to their failure earlier to meet the educational requirement, as well as the age test, for an employment certificate.

Once again it is important to call attention to the differences in the various trades and occupations which are grouped together in the table.* As we have noted, of all the girls included in the investigation, 54 per cent had left school at the age of fourteen or younger, and in manufacturing the proportion was 65 per cent. Some of the industries in which the proportion reporting this early ending of their school days was larger than the average in manufacturing, were the making of men's clothing, 78 per cent; work on confectionery, tobacco,

* See Appendix I, Tables H and J, pp. 199, 201.

and food products, 67 per cent; the white goods trade, 70 per cent; textile manufacture, 68 per cent; and paper box making, 76 per cent.

Likewise, differences appear in the diverse occupational groups listed under the general name of trade and transportation. For the whole group, the proportion leaving school at fourteen or younger was 49 per cent. For workers in stores this proportion was much greater than the average, 61 per cent; for stenographers and bookkeepers it was less, 45 per cent; and for general clerical workers without a knowledge of stenography, 47 per cent. These figures are precisely what one might expect from a knowledge of the educational requirements now generally prevailing for girls in these various occupations. Desirable as it will be some day to have the rank and file of salesgirls and even cash girls better trained for their work, it is a matter of observation that at present the girl who is to survive as a stenographer must stay in school longer than must a salesgirl. Why the trades listed in the preceding paragraph demand so much less of their workers in the way of previous schooling than do other manufacturing pursuits is not equally clear, although it is a matter of common opinion that these industries offer mainly unskilled and poorly paid work to women.

The occupations in which it is apparently easy for young workers to secure a foothold may be discovered by studying the age grouping in the different lines of work represented in the evening schools.* Those occupations having the largest proportion of workers under sixteen were employment in stores, 38 per cent; artificial flower making, 36 per cent; textile manufacture, 33 per cent; button making, 33 per cent; paper box making, 33 per cent; the preparation of hair goods, 32 per cent; and the making of confectionery, food products, and tobacco, 31 per cent. As might be anticipated, these are also the industries employing a large proportion of girls who left school while in the lower grades.

The groups in which the proportion of girls under sixteen is smallest were professional work, 2.1 per cent; stenography, 6.1 per cent; shirtwaist making, 11 per cent; dressmaking, 15 per cent; clerical work, 18 per cent; manufacturing white goods, 19 per cent; and making men's clothing, 20 per cent. In general, these are occupations which require a special equipment or trades which employ machine operators in large numbers.

At present, children between the ages of fourteen and sixteen are the subject of special discussion by school authorities and investigators in many communities. In New York City alone somewhat more than 40,000 children apply for employment certificates in a year, of whom approximately 20,000 are girls. The exodus of thousands from the seventh grade or earlier is a fact so well established as to receive a special title, "mortality in

* Appendix I, Table G, p. 198.

the elementary grades." The fact causes concern not only because it indicates premature ending of the school career, but because these are the children who are immediately absorbed by the industries of the city. They are facing at a critical age all the difficulties of transition from school to work. Investigators of industry have been piling up evidence to show that usually the work which fourteen- and fifteen-year-old children do is not educational, nor is it the first rung of the ladder of success. School careers are cut short for an industrial experience which proves later to be a positive handicap in the effort to find a really good job. But quite aside from the industrial conditions which a fourteen-year-old wage-earner encounters, her employment raises the question: Is it best for the child and the community that she should go to work at all before the sixteenth birthday, and what conditions are driving young children into the labor market?

Naturally the first answer which comes to mind is that children go to work because their families need their earnings. Much time has been spent by several investigators* to discover how many

* Diversity in the findings of investigators indicates the difficulties in the way of accuracy. Among other reports on this subject may be mentioned:

Flexner, Mary: A Plea for Vocational Training. *The Survey*, XXII: 650–655 (August 7, 1909). No estimate made by the author. Apparently 380 out of a total of 530, or 72 per cent, left school because of economic pressure.

Adams, Jessie B.: The Working Girl from the Elementary School in New York. *Charities and The Commons*, XIX: 1617 (February 22, 1908).—"That 'money was needed' was voluntarily given as a reason children who leave school for work at the age of fourteen do so because of so-called economic pressure. The determination is a difficult one, primarily because no one yet knows just how to measure economic pressure. Presumably it is the difference between the actual income and the amount necessary to maintain an adequate stand-

more often than any other, and a real need for the child's earnings often exists."

Report on Condition of Woman and Child Wage-Earners in the United States. Vol. VII, Conditions under which Children Leave School to Go to Work, p. 46. United States Senate Document No. 645.—The table shows that out of a total of 620, 186 (30 per cent) left school because of economic pressure.

United States Bureau of Education, Bulletin No. 17, 1913. Whole number 525. A Trade School for Girls: A Preliminary Investigation in a Typical Manufacturing City, Worcester, Mass., p. 27.—"Of 214 families studied, fully one-half the girls were not forced to curtail their education, and 55 per cent were living in really comfortable homes."

Report of the Massachusetts Commission on Industrial and Technical Education, April, 1906.—"Forty per cent of these families declared they wanted their children to remain in school; and what is more tragic, 66 per cent of them could have kept them there." (p. 44.)

"The report of those who left school from necessity is 2,450 out of 5,459" (44 per cent). (P. 86.)

Talbert, Ernest L.: Opportunities in School and Industry for Children of the Stockyards District, p. 14. Chicago, University of Chicago Press, 1912.—"Out of this number (330), 171 (52 per cent) gave lack of money as the prime cause of leaving school."

Barrows, Alice P.: Report of the Vocational Guidance Survey, December, 1912, p. 7. Public Education Association Bulletin 9, reprinted from the Fourteenth Annual Report of the City Superintendent of Schools, New York City, 1912.—"On the basis of the government's standard of income, only 20 per cent of the children *had* to leave on account of economic pressure."

Woolley, Helen T.: Charting Childhood in Cincinnati. *The Survey*, XXX: 601 (August 9, 1913).—"Only 27 per cent of the families were believed to require the earnings of the children, while 73 per cent had apparently no such economic need."

Superintendent of Schools, New York City. Fourteenth Annual Report, 1911–12. Report on Evening Schools for the Year Ending July 31, 1912, p. 75.—"Seventy per cent of a thousand boys, therefore, did not leave school voluntarily."

ard of living. But the amount necessary for an adequate standard of living is not yet scientifically established. Furthermore, the task of determining the actual income in a wage-earner's household is delicate and often impossible, since amid all the fluctuations in employment the wage-earner himself does not know how much his earnings amount to in a year. Therefore, the measurement of economic pressure depends on a comparison of two indeterminate quantities. In reality, it is one phase of the difficult task of measuring the extent of poverty in a community. In the absence of more scientific data, the statements of the children themselves and their parents throw light on the situation. After all, the members of the family know better than an outsider whether or not they feel economic pressure.

This was the informal method followed in questioning 108 girls who had left school before the age of sixteen, and who were interviewed at home in the course of our investigation. As many as 90 of these girls were the product of New York public schools, 18 having recently left parochial school. Sixteen of those who had been pupils in a public school in New York had reached the eighth grade, 16 had graduated, and seven had gone to high school for brief periods. The remaining 51, a large majority in a group of 90, had left school while in the seventh grade or earlier. The reasons why they left school before they were sixteen, as stated by the girls and their parents, are

TABLE 22.—REASONS FOR LEAVING DAY SCHOOL BEFORE THE AGE OF SIXTEEN, FOR 108 GIRLS ATTENDING PUBLIC EVENING SCHOOLS[a]

Reason for leaving day school	GIRLS WHO LEFT SCHOOL WHEN ATTENDING NEW YORK PUBLIC SCHOOLS		Girls who left school when attending New York parochial schools	All girls
	Before graduation from elementary school	At graduation or after entering high school		
Girls' earnings necessary at home:				
Family could not afford to let her stay	33	8	8	49
Father ill, out of work	3	2	..	5
Total	36	10	8	54
All other reasons:				
To help others to get an education	1	2	..	3
Parents wished her to stop	2	..	..	2
Wished to go to work	3	2	..	5
Had begun work in vacation	1	..	1	2
Backward and family took her out, or advised by teachers to leave	9	..	1	10
Disagreed with teacher	1	..	1	2
Thought graduation time to leave, or saw no advantage in staying	6	2	5	13
To go to business school, no higher grade in the school, discouraged, course too long, another year added	2	2	1	5
Because other girls left	2	..	1	3
Not strong	1	5	..	6
Needed at home	3	..	..	3
Total	31	13	10	54
Grand total	67	23	18	108

[a] Based on the statements of the girls and their parents.

listed in Table 22. In several instances more than one reason was assigned, but the one which seemed predominant was selected for the table.

Exactly half the number said that they left school to go to work because their earnings were needed at home. The others assigned varied reasons, some of them trivial, but most of them significant. Marion, who was spending her days in an embroidery factory cutting out lace, left because she did not care for study and her mother thought it was useless to force her to be a student. Sarah, in contrast, had wanted to be educated. "I was very smart in school but I lost interest when my mother was sick. When someone is sick at home your brain is at home."

For Mabel, a little messenger in a very large department store, the reason for leaving school was not obscure. She applied for working papers on her fourteenth birthday. "Some people can afford to keep their children in school but where there's so many you can't," said her tired mother, while four babies, aged one, three, five, and seven, tugged at her skirts. She was preparing a meager lunch for them and for three others who were in school. Mabel was the oldest. For hard work in a butcher shop the father was earning $12 a week, a wage which did not stretch far over the needs of eight children. The children all looked anemic, with weak eyes like their mother's. Mabel could not learn a trade because of poor eyesight, her mother explained. "We tried living in the country

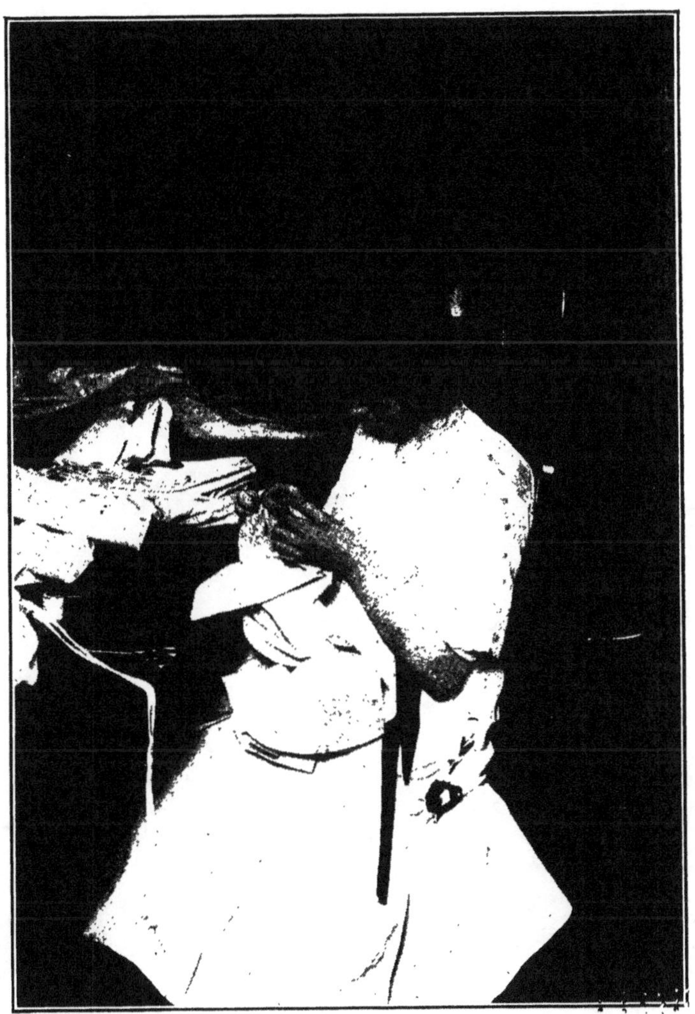

In the Pattern Drafting Class

once," said she. "We heard so much about its being better for the children. We were two years on Long Island, but we couldn't get along at all. My husband was out of work and we got discouraged."

Mabel worked hard. She traveled from 123d Street and First Avenue to Sixth Avenue and Thirty-fourth Street, leaving home a few minutes before 7 a.m. From 8 in the morning until 6 at night, nine and one-quarter hours besides the three-quarters of an hour recess at noon, she served as messenger at the beck and call of the saleswomen in the huge department store, which paid her a wage of $3.50 a week. Reaching home for a hasty meal, she must hurry off for her walk 18 blocks to the south and three to the west, more than a mile, to evening school. "She gets home after ten," said her mother. "She's very tired at night."

It should be observed that Mabel was not an orphan nor the sole support of a widowed mother. In this respect she was like the majority of the 108 girls under sixteen who, as outlined in Chapter III, were questioned about long hours of work. Seven of these girls were boarding or living with relatives who were not members of their immediate family, while 101 were in their own homes, and in 77 of these homes the father was at work and contributing to the family income. In 16 of the 24 other households the father was dead, in two he had deserted, and in six he was ill or "too old to work." In 15 families the mother was a wage-earner outside the home, and in four she earned money by janitor service in the tenement in which the family lived. The noteworthy fact here is that in three-fourths of these families of fourteen-year-old wage-earners the fathers were at work. If the earnings of the children were really necessary, it is a significant comment on the wages paid their fathers.

The statistics of a larger group of evening school pupils give some indirect evidence as to whether all the children who leave school early do so in order to become wage-earners. Of 2,632 girls under sixteen in evening schools, 803, or nearly one in three, made no reply to the question: What do you do?* In some cases, as already pointed out in an earlier chapter, this may have been a careless omission. It should be remembered, however, that one condition of entrance to evening school is inability to attend day school, and these young girls, knowing this fact, would have been likely to record their occupations if they had had any. Furthermore, the compulsory education law requires children between fourteen and sixteen to attend day school if they are not at work. In some cases the evening school record contained some such definite statement as "never employed." Moreover, at that age a girl is proud of being a wage-earner and likely to take every opportunity to tell others that she is at work. For all these reasons, and because home visits to a number of these evening school girls have resulted in corrobo-

* See Appendix I, Table G, p. 198.

ration of the records, it seems safe to assume that the facts are substantially correct; namely, that these girls were not at work and that whatever may have been the reasons for leaving day school, the certainty of an immediate job was not one of them. This seems to indicate that the day schools are losing girls under sixteen who have no occupation in view and no intention of going to work immediately. Economic pressure is evidently not the controlling motive for these girls.

The function of the evening schools in making good the deficiencies in early schooling has been recognized for many years, and wage-earners have joined the classes with this purpose very definitely in view. A study of these evening school pupils reveals information significant for the elementary schools. For instance, full recognition of the fact that for the present, at least, eight or nine years only can be spared for the entire school life of thousands of children should undoubtedly lead to good results for the elementary schools. By placing in the lower grades the best teaching force available, a fair proportion of the children who now drop out too early might be induced to stay longer, while for others the eight or nine years of schooling, brief as it is, might be made more valuable.

Furthermore, if vocational courses of any kind are to be taught in schools of elementary grade, the evening schools, through their contact with many wage-earners of the present, may well become guides for the day schools in their education of the workers of the future. They may serve as guides not only by providing the sort of information which this investigation, for example, has shown to be forthcoming from evening school pupils, but they may actually experiment in industrial courses. Some of the problems involved in developing vocational courses in the evening schools will be discussed in the following chapter.

CHAPTER V

RELATION OF THE EVENING SCHOOLS TO VOCATIONAL TRAINING

AS experiment stations in vocational training, the evening schools have one advantage over the day schools, in that the majority of the pupils in evening classes have already a basis of experience in wage-earning pursuits. This advantage has been potential, however, rather than actual, since in most cases the pupils have been enrolled in classes in which the instruction bore no relation to their daily occupations. This has been due partly to the inclination of the pupils, but chiefly to the fact that until recently no effort was made to offer training which should really supplement the experience gained in factory and workshop.

On the other hand, the evening schools can never fulfill the functions of day trade schools, if for no other reason than for lack of time. The total time spent in actual work during a winter in New York is ninety evenings, or one hundred and eighty hours, in the elementary evening schools and one hundred and twenty evenings, or two hundred and forty hours, in the high schools. Assuming that nine hours is the usual working day, this means that the whole winter's work of an evening class in an elementary school is equivalent to twenty days in industry and in a high school to twenty-six days and six hours. The disadvantage of lack of time and the advantage of utilizing the daily experience of the pupils alike indicate the possible function of evening classes as means of supplementary training in a scheme of vocational education.

Massachusetts, in its plan of state aid for evening industrial schools, recognizes this condition as determining the legitimate scope of these schools.* The state gives financial aid only in case the evening courses are intended for persons already employed by day in the same trades taught in the evening, "to the end," as the statute says, "that instruction in the principles and the practices of the arts may go on together." The factory girl, domestic servant, or housewife who seeks instruction to make her more efficient in her work is welcome to join a class made up of others in the same occupation, because she already has the practice related to the principles to be taught in the class. On the other hand, the domestic servant who wishes to be trained for factory work, the shop girl who wishes to learn cooking, or the saleswoman who wants to trim her own hats, is not admitted

* National Society for the Promotion of Industrial Education, Bulletin No. 13. Proceedings, Fourth Annual Convention, 1910. Part III, Part Time and Evening Schools. Address by C. A. Prosser on Massachusetts Independent Evening Industrial Schools, pp. 129–143.

to the classes intended for those actually employed in factories or households or millinery shops, for the very practical reason that in so short a time the aim which the pupil herself has in view could not be accomplished, since she is not gaining experience in these occupations by day.

In New York the requirements for entrance to evening industrial classes have not been so strict. The vocational classes for women have included courses in stenography, bookkeeping, costume design, millinery, dressmaking, and cooking. In some instances a class in stenography, a "speed" class, for instance, has been limited to those already employed in that occupation. In the so-called home-making courses, however—millinery, dressmaking, and cooking—the classes have been made up chiefly of those who wanted to gain practice in one of these arts as a personal accomplishment. Milliners, dressmakers, or cooks, were few in number in these class rooms, since the courses were not planned to meet their needs. Sometimes a girl would join the class under the impression that if she completed the course she could earn her living as a dressmaker or milliner. In some instances what she learned did help her to gain entrance to the trade, but the practice was too brief and the plan of work too little adapted to trade needs to make her a skilled worker. These classes have been dominated by the idea of teaching the art for "home use," and it is obvious that the girl who takes her own materials to class and slowly makes and trims a hat for herself is not thereby qualified for the demands of a modern millinery establishment.

The working out of courses limited chiefly to girls who have had actual experience in trade, and planned to meet their special needs, is illustrated by the evening classes organized in the spring of 1913 in the Manhattan Trade School for Girls. In equipment, in courses offered, in requirements for entrance, in choice of teachers, and in general plan of work, the experiment is suggestive.

The Manhattan Trade School is a day school for girls, which was started in 1902 by private enterprise and was supported for a number of years by private contributions. Later, in the year 1910, it became part of the public school system of New York. The courses offered included dressmaking, millinery, lamp-shade making and other novelty work, and machine operating of various kinds, such as plain sewing, embroidery with special machines, and straw hat making. These were all planned to instruct girls who intended to be wage-earners in these trades.

The equipment of these day classes determined the courses to be offered in the evening. The long machines, operated by electric power, were ready for four classes—elementary machine operating for various branches of the clothing trade, advanced work in the same occupation, machine embroidery, and straw hat making. The dressmaking rooms, with cutting tables, figures for draping, and so forth, were utilized for two classes, one in pattern drafting and cutting, and one in waist draping. For lamp-shade making, no special tools other than needles are necessary, but the long tables and the movable chairs were similar to those used in workrooms. The task of relating the courses to trade requirements was thus greatly simplified by the furnishing of the rooms, in refreshing contrast to the small desks, clamped to the floor, which cause such discomfort in many evening schools.

No girl was permitted to enter one of these evening classes unless she was definitely and purposefully seeking training for wage-earning. To take the course in advanced machine operating, in machine embroidery, or in straw sewing, actual trade experience in plain machine operating was required. If the applicant had had no such experience, she might be enrolled in the elementary class in machine operating, and look forward later to the possibility of learning straw sewing or machine embroidery. Only girls actually employed in dressmaking establishments* were admitted to the classes in waist draping or in pattern drafting. This careful sifting of applicants made possible a unity of purpose in the class rooms which added

* As will be shown later, the exceptions to this rule included three workers in shirtwaist making,—an occupation, however, which is a branch of wholesale dressmaking,—one neckwear maker who had formerly worked in dressmaking, one operator of an embroidery machine, one employed in a clothing factory, and one student who had taken the day course in the Manhattan Trade School and was helping in the school by day. (Table 23, p. 130.)

much to the efficiency of the instruction. Equally careful was the selection of teachers. Definite trade experience and the personality needed for effective teaching were the chief factors in the choice.

The same careful consideration of the daily work of pupils and teachers alike was shown in the plan to have each class meet two nights instead of four, thus making regularity of attendance more possible. Furthermore, supper was served at cost in the school so that girls might come direct from their work without first taking a long trip home for a hurried dinner. Attendance, too, was encouraged by so planning the courses as to give the instruction in 30 lessons during a short period of fifteen weeks. The pupils could thus see the end of the course from the beginning and could mark their progress in it as the days passed.

The courses in waist draping and in pattern drafting and cutting may be described more fully as illustrative of the idea implied in the Massachusetts law already discussed,—the combination of practice by day and instruction in principles in the evening. In waist draping the aim was to develop facility and accuracy in modeling a waist from a design shown in a sketch on paper. The course in pattern drafting and cutting was planned not to afford practice in the art but to teach fundamental principles of line and measurement in the making of a dress.

"We do not expect the girls to draft patterns in

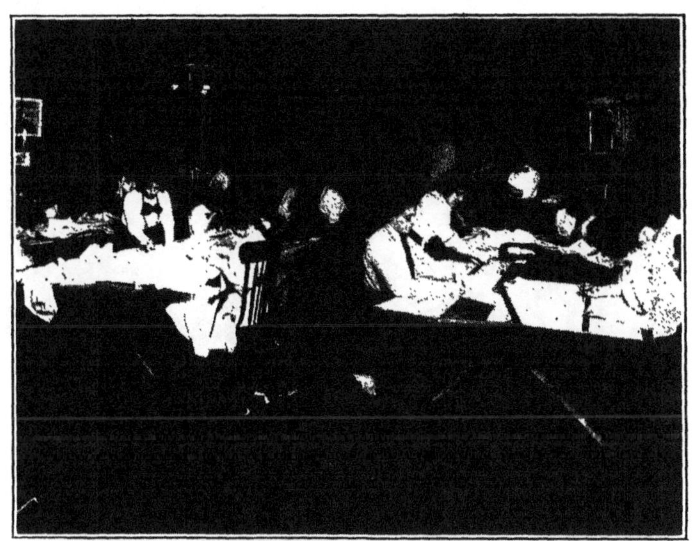

Pattern Drafting
Manhattan Evening Trade School

Waist Draping for Dressmakers

the workroom," said the principal. "Pattern drafting for dressmakers is like psychology for teachers. The teacher may not make direct use of her knowledge of psychology, but its principles should underlie all her work."

In the trade itself, instruction in underlying principles is not usual; for dressmaking, like many other occupations, has felt the influence of machinery and subdivision of labor. This condition is reflected in the records of the 699 dressmakers attending the various evening schools, who were included in the investigation.* A few worked at home or by the day for private customers; others were in large or small custom shops; and a third group worked in wholesale dressmaking factories. The dressmaker who works for her own customers is an all-round worker to whom subdivision of processes is unknown. At the other extreme is the girl who can not accurately be called a dressmaker; she is a hand in a large factory. The processes named by shop employes included designing, draping, waist making and waist finishing, skirt making and skirt finishing, skirt draping, sewing in linings, hemming, tucking, pressing, examining, folding, and such minor tasks as cutting out embroidery, pinking, taking out bastings, and distributing work. Others were forewomen and one owner of a shop was included.

Two comments may be made on this list. Skilled

* Study of the Manhattan Trade School evening classes was not, of course, included in our original investigation, as these were not organized until 1913.

processes of high rank, like designing and draping, are open to women, and it is by no means unusual for women to own and manage shops. Furthermore, in many specialized tasks skill is required, as in tucking, waist and skirt making, and the like. On the other hand, with so marked a subdivision of processes as is found in large establishments, many workers must be too absorbed in repetition of simple tasks to gain any knowledge of the principles necessary to make them eligible for positions ahead. It was to meet just such a need that the evening courses in the Manhattan Trade School were planned.

The need thus outlined in general was voiced very definitely by the girls who were attending these classes. One girl, for instance, had worked in the trade five years in New York City, and before coming here she had served a two years' apprenticeship in Budapest. She was earning $9.00 a week in a wholesale dressmaking shop but had never had an opportunity to try any process except finishing. Her work on the dresses began after they had been cut and draped. She saw no chance to get ahead unless she could learn draping in an evening school.

The story of this girl is worth telling. She had attended another evening school in New York four years to learn to speak English. She could read it before she left Hungary, and the list of languages which she could speak included also Hungarian, Italian, Roumanian, German, Spanish, and a little French. In Budapest, she had not only served an apprenticeship in dressmaking but had learned bookkeeping. She had held a position as bookkeeper for three years after she reached the United States. Then she thought she could earn more as a dressmaker. She had come all alone at the age of seventeen and had no relatives here. She was boarding and was entirely dependent on her own earnings. The grit and determination of this girl to advance would be inspiring were not one disheartened by the realization of how little use the industrial world had made of her talents.

Two other ambitious girls in the waist draping class were waist finishers in a retail shop. They were attending regularly, so that at the first opportunity in the shop they might become assistant drapers and later, drapers. Meanwhile, they were hoping that an evening class in designing would be started in order that they might take another step forward.

In the next room, learning pattern drafting, was a girl who had already gone part way up the ladder these younger workers were hoping to scale. She was a draper in a retail shop, earning $12 a week. Her advice was to learn pattern drafting first as a foundation for designing. She was taking the course with just that purpose in view; namely, to become a designer. Her training in the trade had been secured under difficulties. As a child, she had never learned to sew, and in her first job in a dressmaking establishment she was paid 50 cents a week. It took three years to arrive at a wage of $5.00. At the time when she was interviewed she was boarding and, in spite of her wage of $12, found the seasonal problem a difficult one. She wished that the evening schools would offer courses to enable every girl in a season trade to be trained in a supplementary occupation for use in dull season.

Another girl in the same class told of an interesting position she might have secured the week before at $18 a week if she had had more of just the training she was receiving in pattern drafting. The work was offered by a dressmaking firm whose customers order their gowns by correspondence and never appear at the shop for a fitting. A worker was needed who would be expert in making dresses from measurements sent by mail. This girl was not yet expert enough, but hoped to become so. Meanwhile, the course helped her in her present position, where she altered gowns according to measurements given in writing.

A bright, vivacious young Italian girl of nineteen, in the pattern drafting and cutting class, told us quite simply and enthusiastically about her trade career and her plans for the future. She had learned machine operating in the day course of the Manhattan Trade School and had left two years and two months before to become a machine operator at $6.00 a week in a wholesale dressmaking establishment. She did so well that in a year she became a maker of model dresses. She was earning $15, making chiffon dresses as samples for the other workers to copy. She had learned in the shop to drape the dresses she made, so she did not need the course in waist draping, but she did need that in pattern drafting and cutting. She wanted to know more about line and measurement, for she intended to fit herself to be a designer. Meanwhile, in addition to her regular work, she made dresses at home for private customers.

In the same class was a colored girl who went out by the day as a dressmaker for private customers. She, too, had been trained in the day course of the Manhattan Trade School, afterward working in a shop as an assistant waist finisher. If she was to be really efficient as a dressmaker dealing directly with her own customers, she felt that she must understand how to draft patterns and cut, as much for the knowledge these would give her of the whole art of dressmaking as for the actual use of the processes in her daily work.

The following outline of the lessons in the class in waist draping shows that the emphasis was not on practice which the girls already have in full measure in the shops, but on fundamental principles which they have difficulty in acquiring in a workroom.

MANHATTAN EVENING TRADE SCHOOL

Course in Waist Draping*

30 Lessons

1. Study of fashion plates and discussion of lines in waists. Demonstration and criticism of several models.
2. Preparation of lining, padding of lining on the figure.

3–4. Practice draping with tissue paper, several different models.

5–6. Practice draping (one model) with cambric or cheesecloth in two different colors.

7–8. Fitting net on yoke and collar.

9–19. Draping waist in cloth.

20–30. Draping waist in silk with chiffon or lace.

To those unfamiliar with the mysteries of dressmaking, the significance of this outline may be obscure. Suffice it to say that the girl who understands how to drape the whole waist and make it like the model will know better how to make or finish a sleeve, or how to baste a lining. This fact will be quite convincing to any woman who with the help only of an inexperienced seamstress has

* Each girl is required to work with a figure and the effort is made to get all preparatory work (such as making linings, sewing, and getting materials ready to drape) done outside of the class period, so that the class period may be devoted to the artistic and creative side.

struggled to reproduce an alluring model pictured in a fashion magazine. Far more than the careful use of the needle is required to make a gown, even if the picture is before one's eyes.

It is no new thing to have a dressmaking class in an evening school in New York, but this is the first time that one has been planned to meet definitely and exclusively the needs of girls already in the trade. Hitherto, as has been stated, the aim has been to teach women to make clothes for themselves or their families. Necessarily the courses have been planned to give brief practice in fashioning various kinds of garments,—beginning with corset covers and shirtwaists, and ending perhaps with a lined dress of chiffon. Obviously there is neither time nor adequate experience for study of line, measurement, or design. These courses given in the night schools, however, are so often spoken of as industrial or vocational that they are likely to be an obstacle in the development of real industrial education, unless the difference between them and the instruction needed by girls in the trade be clearly understood.

Jennie, for instance, was an errand girl in a large wholesale dressmaking establishment. She was "ambitious to learn all about the dressmaking trade," as she expressed it. She began to go from shop to shop, gaining a little different experience in each position. "They say that a rolling stone gathers no moss, but I would never advance if I didn't change my position." She was eager to know where she could find a class in designing, as that was her goal in her trade. This was a year before the Manhattan Trade School evening classes had been organized. Jennie attended an evening school, but she had entered a class in business English and bookkeeping rather than the class in dressmaking. "What can one teacher and two old machines do in a class of 30 girls?" was her very sagacious comment.

Lucy, a young Italian girl, objected also to the lack of enough machines. She joined a dressmaking class and left it in less than a month. "I didn't like it," she said. "I knew more than the teacher and I never could get at the machine. I had to sew everything by hand. I could get more done at home." For much the same reason Irene, a stock girl in a department store, left evening school. "She could run up two of those corset covers on the machine at home while she was making one at school by hand," said her mother.

If these criticisms are well founded, it is peculiarly unfortunate that classes intended to train girls in the arts of home making, including sewing, should not demonstrate the principle of accomplishing tasks efficiently by using always the proper tools.

At their best, however, the class in home arts and the class in trade practice are so unlike as to make it necessary to separate them, admitting to the trade class only the girls who are wage-earners or intend to be, and letting it be clearly understood that the home class offers no experience of real value in a workshop. For in the class intended to train girls to sew well at home the individual foot-treadle machines should be used; while for trade work, a girl must know how to run a power machine.

In order to get more light on this experiment in the Manhattan Trade School, we made a special study of the application schedules filled out by the girls who entered the classes. The daily occupations of the 195 girls enrolled in 1913 are shown in Table 23.

The classes in elementary machine operating and in lamp-shade work, as already explained, were the only ones to which girls not experienced in an allied process were admitted. Two milliners took the course in lamp-shade making, probably to enable them to find work when the millinery trade was slack. The similarity between making a hat and making a lamp shade is apparent when one reflects that both have some kind of a frame as a foundation and similar materials are used; both need hand sewing with various fancy stitches similar in kind, such as slip-stitching, facing, shirring, and making frills; and both demand accurate perception of line and form. In the day classes in the Manhattan Trade School every milliner is now required to learn lamp-shade making as a possible solution of the seasonal problem later to be encountered in the millinery trade.

TABLE 23.—DAILY OCCUPATIONS OF WOMEN ATTENDING EVENING CLASSES IN THE MANHATTAN TRADE SCHOOL BY CLASSES, NEW YORK CITY, 1913

Occupation	Women attending classes in							All women
	Elem. plain operating	Adv. plain operating	Straw sewing	Embr'd'y machine operating	Waist draping	Drafting, cutting, fitting	Lamp-shade making	
Dressmaking—women's, children's and infants'	..	3	6	3	26	55	..	93
Shirtwaist making	..	2	..	..	1	2	..	5
Underwear, men's and women's, making of	..	5	5	..	..	..	..	10
Neckwear, men's and women's, making of	..	2	5	1	..	1	..	9
Corset making	..	1	..	..	..	..	..	1
Bathing suits, making of	..	1	..	..	..	..	..	1
Shirt making	..	..	1	..	..	..	..	1
Clothing not otherwise specified, making of	2	8	6	5	..	1	..	22
Millinery and making of children's hats	..	5	7	..	..	..	2	14
Straw sewing	..	1	..	4	..	..	..	5
Embroidery—hand, machine, and bonnaz	..	1	1	4	..	1	1	8
Work on furs	..	2	..	..	..	..	..	2
Curtain making	..	1	..	..	..	..	..	1
Candy making	1	..	..	..	..	..	..	1
Tobacco, work on	2	..	..	..	..	..	..	2
Post cards, work on	..	..	..	..	..	..	1	1
Burnishing	..	..	..	..	..	..	1	1
Office work and stenography	4	..	..	..	..	..	1	5
Sales work	4	..	..	..	..	..	1	5
Waitress work	..	..	..	..	..	..	1	1
No occupation stated	5	..	..	..	1	..	1	7
Total	18	32	31	17	28	60	9	195

Process	Women attending classes in							All women
	Elem. plain operating	Adv. plain operating	Straw sewing	Embr'd'y machine operating	Waist draping	Drafting, cutting, fitting	Lamp-shade making	
Operating	2	6	21	15	..	4	..	48
Hand sewing	..	11	7	2	18	16	3	57
Examining	..	4	..	..	..	..	..	4
Stock keeping	..	6	..	..	1	..	..	7
Cutting	..	..	..	..	..	1	..	1
Draping	..	..	..	..	2	..	..	2
Designing	..	..	..	..	..	1	..	1
Miscellaneous, or process not specified	11	5	3	..	6	38	5	68
No occupation stated	5	..	..	..	1	..	1	7
Total	18	32	31	17	28	60	9	195

In the class in advanced machine operating every girl was employed by day in some industry in which the power machine is used, including the making of curtains, furs, millinery, straw hats, neckwear, underwear, shirtwaists, corsets, machine embroidery, women's clothing, and bathing suits. The daily work of six of these girls was machine operating; that of 11, hand sewing; in addition there were four examiners and six stock girls. The machine operators wanted more skill, and the hand workers, including examiners and stock girls, wanted a chance, usually denied them in the workrooms where "no learners are employed," to practice on machines so that they could be transferred to machine processes and earn higher wages. With very few exceptions, the girls in waist draping and pattern drafting classes were employed in the dressmaking trade.

Not only young workers were attracted to these classes. Table 24, which gives ages, indicates that many of them had probably had several years' experience as wage-earners. Their decision to attend evening school to acquire more training was therefore the more significant of the need which they felt, and of the failure of the industries themselves to provide adequate training.

Only four were under sixteen and two of these passed the sixteenth birthday while taking the course. More than a third, 73, were twenty-one or over. But it may be inferred by some that the age alone is no proof of need of training on the part

Machine Operating
Manhattan Evening Trade School

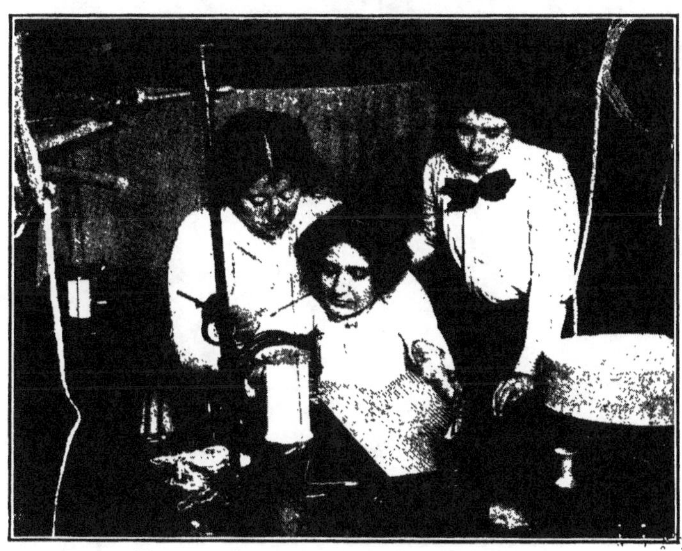

Teacher Instructing in Straw Sewing

of wage-earners in general, since these girls who attended the Manhattan Evening Trade School may have been failures in their occupations. On this point, the evidence adduced from their wages is important. The data appear in Table 25.

The census of 1905 told us that the average weekly earnings of women in all manufacturing

TABLE 24.—AGES OF WOMEN ATTENDING EVENING CLASSES IN THE MANHATTAN TRADE SCHOOL, NEW YORK CITY, 1913

Age	Women of the ages specified
Less than 16 years	4
16 years and less than 18 years	57
18 years and less than 21 years	57
21 years and less than 25 years	38
25 years and less than 35 years	23
35 years and less than 45 years	11
45 years or more	1
Total	191[a]

[a] Of 195 women, four did not supply information.

pursuits grouped together in New York State was $6.54.* Gauged by that fact, the wages of these girls attending the Manhattan Trade School in the evening were well above the average. For the whole group, the average was $8.42, and for those of twenty-one years or older, $9.88. A further classification in wage groups showed that 77, or 44 per cent, were earning less than $8.00, and 97, or

* United States Census, Bulletin 93, Earnings of Wage-Earners, Manufactures, p. 150. 1905.

56 per cent, were earning $8.00 or more, with 19, or 11 per cent, earning between $12 and $15, and four, or 2.3 per cent, earning $15 or over. That at the very beginning of this experiment girls who, as wages go, are among the more highly paid, should be taking advantage of these new night classes,

TABLE 25.—AVERAGE WEEKLY WAGES, BY AGES, OF WOMEN ATTENDING EVENING CLASSES IN THE MANHATTAN TRADE SCHOOL, NEW YORK CITY, 1913

Age	Women reporting wages	Average weekly wage
Less than 16 years	4	$4.25
16 years and less than 18 years	56	6.56
18 years and less than 21 years	51	8.93
21 years and less than 25 years	35	10.13
25 years or more	27	9.57
Not stated	1	12.50
Total	174[a]	$8.42
18 years or more	113	$9.45
21 years or more	62	9.88

[a] Of the 195 women, 14 did not report wages and seven had no occupation or stated none.

speaks well for the general efficiency of the plan of work. On the other hand, it shows to what an extent all-round training is neglected in the work-rooms, since girls who evidently have an assured foothold in their occupations have not been able to secure in the shops the training for which they feel the need.

Less than 200 girls were enrolled in these

classes, and the scope of the courses was strictly limited. It is too early to judge of the results which may show themselves in the future trade careers of these girls. The effect of the methods, however, was visible in the atmosphere of the class rooms; in the quickened interest of the pupils in every process of their occupations, an interest often deadened in workrooms by monotony and by discouraging and fatiguing conditions.

The successful operation of these classes seems to indicate the possible function of the evening schools in giving supplementary training to girls in many different occupations. But the experiment should not be limited to classes in dressmaking and the allied trades. At the risk of boring a patient reader, it seems well to drive home a realization of the great complexity of the industrial problem which we are considering by reciting in detail some of the actual occupations of girls in New York. For example, what shall be done for the flower and feather makers; for the makers of men's clothing, of boys' suits and overcoats, of vests, shirts, men's neckwear, collars and cuffs, suspenders, and caps; for the makers of women's tailored garments, of shirtwaists, petticoats and underwear; neckwear, corsets, bathing suits, kimonos, aprons, wrappers, dressing sacks; and of children's dresses, underwear and caps; for the workers who dip chocolate, wrap, pack, and label candies, stamp and pack chewing gum, fill boxes with licorice; or pack, label, and seal all kinds of bakery products, canned vegetables, preserved fruits, noodles, corn beef, olives, butter and eggs, yeast cakes, salad oil, tea, sugar, spices and coffee, and make and pack cigars and cigarettes; for the girls who operate, perforate, line, finish, cover, make buttonholes, put on beading, and perform many other processes of shoe manufacture; for the workers in the glove factories who operate machines, trim, steam, put on clasps, reel silk, spin, bind, and, of course, examine and pack; for the makers of leather belts, purses, dress shields, rain coats, trusses, garters and other goods of rubber; for the workers on fur and makers of mattresses; for the numerous employes in the recently prosperous hair goods industry; for the makers of articles of bone and pearl and horn, of feather dusters and cushions, fans, mirrors, jewelry cases and badges; for milliners and makers of embroidered articles of many kinds and materials; for makers of handkerchiefs, sheets, pillow cases, tablecloths, flags, quilts, burial robes, ribbon novelties, umbrella covers and strips of buttonholes purchasable for home dressmaking; for girls employed in bookbinding, the manufacture of stationery, lithographing, paper box making, printing, making paper bags and sample cards; for workers in a diverse list of processes needed in the manufacture of cotton goods, braids, and passementerie, knit goods, including sweaters, stockings and underwear, lace and veils, silk goods, carpets, woolen goods, upholstery goods, scarfs and shawls, window shades, bags, mats, and other articles of flax, hemp or jute; for the wage-earning girls who in seeking their livelihood seem to have departed far from women's sphere in electing to work on products of stone, clay, glass, and metal, from the packing of fishing tackle to the lacquering of toys and the stamping of glass and china; the testing of electric lights and graphophones, lantern making, wood and cork manufacture, including life preservers, cigar boxes, and toothpicks; the preparation of drugs and chemicals, paints and dyes, soap, perfumery, and candles; work on products of gold, silver, precious stones, and jewelry; the manufacture of lamp shades of copper or glass; the making of dental supplies; and finally for girls engaged in all the processes of cleaning, dyeing, and general laundry work?

The interrogation mark at the end of this list is to be taken in its fullest meaning. The questions involved in industrial education for women will not be answered until we take account of all the diverse trades in which women are employed. Even this lengthy enumeration represents merely a picked list for purposes of illustration. It is not complete even for manufacturing and mechanical pursuits, and it excludes entirely any mention of the many distinct occupations counted under the census headings: domestic and personal service, trade and transportation, agricultural pursuits, and professional work—stenographers and bookkeepers, clerical workers, saleswomen, buyers and shoppers, telephone girls and telegraph operators, manicures, hairdressers, waitresses in restaurants, nurse maids, besides statisticians, librarians, dietitians, interpreters, translators, and teachers. It must be understood that all these illustrations are drawn from the card records of women actually attending public evening schools; that, incomplete as the actual list of occupations is, we have counted on these cards 289 subdivisions of the main occupational groups, and that still further subdivision would be necessary to count the actual number of distinct tasks, each of which represents the day's work of a wage-earning woman.

The evening classes in dressmaking in the Manhattan Trade School were made possible because the school had had experience in training girls for this trade, and its general conditions and processes are known. No one person and no one group of persons, however, has sufficient knowledge as yet to work out parallel courses in any considerable number of other industries. Moreover, what we know of other trades shows us that the problems in them are distinctly different from those in dressmaking. Take, for example, bookbinding. Machines dominate the industry. The line of demarcation between men's work and women's work is sharply drawn. Women are not called upon to plan or to design; their tasks are mechanical and highly specialized. Speed, good team work, and facility in a mechanical process are the chief requirements. Employers and workers alike say that they can see no scope for supplementary schooling with a definite vocational bearing for women in this industry.* This does not mean that all thought of industrial education for women in this trade must be abandoned. It does mean, however, that much study and careful experiment will be necessary to work out any feasible plan.

After all, the whole subject of industrial education, viewed in the light of these facts about wage-earning girls in evening schools, divides itself naturally into distinct problems, according to the general types of work in which women are engaged. Skill is not a simple, invariable quality. In some positions and some occupations the need is for imagination, organizing capacity, and general intelligence, in addition to hand skill; as, for instance, in the work of a designer or the duties of a forewoman. In others, hand skill is pre-eminently required, as in straw sewing, machine embroidery, and the making of lace; and skill here means accuracy and delicacy of touch. In other processes, like sewing on buttons, folding pamphlets, packing candy or operating an envelope machine, it means swiftness of movement. In some work, like the trimming of an expensive hat in a wholesale millinery establishment, accuracy and delicacy of touch, speed, and imagination all are needed.

Just what part the evening schools or the day

* For a full discussion of this subject based on an intensive study of women's work in this trade, see Van Kleeck, Mary: Women in the Bookbinding Trade. Russell Sage Foundation Publication. New York, Survey Associates, 1913.

schools can play in developing the efficiency required in these varied types of work is, indeed, problematical, but even more puzzling is the problem of minimizing the effect upon the individual of occupations which require no real efficiency,—monotonous tasks and odd jobs like putting nuts on cakes in a bakery or pasting chenille dots on veils. Getting rid entirely of such work as separate jobs, either by inventing machines or by absorbing them into other jobs so that no one will have them to do continuously, would seem to be a most obvious and imperative solution. This, however, is part of the business of remaking and reforming industry.

Meanwhile the schools must meet conditions as they are. We need not wait to decide the educational theories of the future, since the workers of the present are voicing their needs more or less explicitly by the very fact of their attendance in evening classes. Diversity of experiment is desirable. The first step is to know accurately what occupations are represented in each evening school, and the second, to bring together at night pupils engaged in similar occupations by day, question them regarding their work, learn the facts about their past schooling and its deficiencies, and thus study their present educational needs.* When such inquiry reveals a demand and a need for supplementary training in practice or principles

* The card records now in use in New York evening schools afford a basis for such a study.

involved in the day's work, the important next steps, if we may judge by such experiments as those described in the Manhattan Evening Trade School, are to define the aim, limit registration to those already employed in the occupation to be taught, provide adequate equipment, and secure a teacher who can give expert instruction. The last of these is the most difficult to provide, and the most important. Indeed, it is doubtful whether anything else is needed to solve the problem of industrial training except pupils with singleness of aim and similarity of experience, and a teacher with knowledge of their occupations, with powers of observation, and the capacity to devise new methods for meeting new conditions.

CHAPTER VI

IRREGULAR ATTENDANCE IN EVENING CLASSES

THE biggest handicap of the evening schools is that their work is done in the evening. Teachers and pupils alike have given their best energies to the day's work. "Tired at night school?" said a fourteen-year-old pupil. "Why, yes, sometimes I go to sleep. I don't like the work I'm doing now (cutting the web of garters), holding the scissors all day; the scissors hurt my hand so, and it's so tiresome cutting all the time. But it was worse when I was at children's caps, on my feet all day. I'm weak on my feet. But I can't stop night school because I'm tired, if I want to get my education. I want to go to evening high and be a stenographer." In spite of such ambition, however, many pupils must leave when the season of overtime in the shops compels them to work late. Others lose interest because, perhaps, the tired teacher has not inspired them with zest for learning. Said Flora, a young Russian milliner, "Night school is different from day school—the teacher is not so serious. Sometimes the girls are noisy and the teacher doesn't teach anything all evening. But other times you learn a little, so it's better than nothing." For such reasons as these and for many others due to the inevitable difficulties of night study, irregular attendance continues to be a baffling problem.

It is a problem, too, with a long history. In 1847, "3,224 scholars" registered in the six schools open in that year for the first time, and the average attendance was only 1,224. In 1850 this discrepancy between registration and average attendance so troubled the school authorities that they employed persons to visit the absentees and ascertain the cause of absence. But this plan accomplished little good in increasing the regularity of attendance, and it was abandoned. In 1865, the school authorities, aroused by the fact that the numbers always declined after the first few weeks, carefully analyzed the defects in the schools. First among them they found a lack of stringent regulations regarding admission; too many young children were registered whose presence kept young men and women away. Then, too, contrary to the original plan, pupils were sometimes admitted who were attending day school. A better method of classification on the basis of age and ability was needed, and a larger number of efficient teachers.

In 1866, to cover some of these defects, registration began a week in advance of the opening of classes; no boys under fourteen and no girls under twelve were admitted; it was required that a responsible person accompany or vouch for all applicants at the time of admission; men teachers were selected for boys' classes, or women who had had at least two years' experience in a boys' grammar school. Finally, the board of education established one new school of higher grade to teach young men mechanical and architectural drawing, higher mathematics, bookkeeping, commercial rules, and other general and vocational subjects.

Improvements were the result, and it was found also that the tendency to diminish hours of labor in industry was giving time and opportunity for mental improvement "to thousands hitherto cut off from such advantages." Nevertheless, several years later, in 1887, the total register was 20,645 and the average attendance, 6,976. In that year the city superintendent recommended an exhaustive investigation of evening schools. He stated that some matters, notably irregularity of attendance, seemed to be beyond the control of the schools; that the organization of junior and senior classes, and the various other new methods recommended, had had no effect on attendance. Several years later, in 1902, the school sessions were reduced from five to four per week, but this change also failed to solve the problem of irregular attendance.

In 1910–11, the year of our investigation, the total number of men and women registered in all the evening schools of the city was 111,996, while the average attendance was only 41,207. Of the number registered in elementary schools, 83,145, slightly more than 2,000 attended every one of the 90 possible evenings of the session; while nearly 37,000 were present less than 60 evenings, and 13,000 others stayed a week or less.* In the high schools the record was even worse, 19,028 of the 28,851 registered attending less than 60 evenings, and only 388 answering the roll call regularly through the 120 evenings of the season.

In the reports for 1911–12 and 1912–13,† the attendance figures are analyzed with special care. Consider, for example, the evening elementary schools. Nearly 8,000 who applied for admission and were assigned to classes never appeared again, a fact representing a serious waste of time and money for clerical work. The total enrollment was 101,557, including all who applied for admission. The total registration, counting only those who actually appeared in a class room at least one night, was 93,840.‡ The average attendance, which is computed by adding together the attendance of every evening and then dividing by the total number of evenings in the school year, was only 34,117.§ When this figure is compared with the total of more than 100,000 who were enrolled, the extent of the problem and the

* Superintendent of Schools, New York City. Thirteenth Annual Report, 1910–11. Report on Evening Schools for the Year Ending July 31, 1911, pp. 9–13.

† Superintendent of Schools, New York City. Fifteenth Annual Report, 1912–13. Report on Evening Schools for the Year Ending July 31, 1913, pp. 8–25.

‡ Ibid., p. 16.

§ Ibid., p. 20.

need for careful analysis of the figures become evident.

For the purpose of comparison between groups, a percentage of attendance is computed, which is the ratio of average attendance, already defined, to average register; that is, the total secured by adding together the number of names on the roll books each evening and dividing by the number of evenings. Thus the average register in 1912–13 was 49,438 as compared with the total of 93,840 who appeared at least one evening. The complicating factor here is that pupils enter any month of the school season, and thus the personnel of the class rooms may undergo more violent changes than an actual count of the number on the books night after night would indicate. The millinery teacher's roll call of 20 pupils in January—the "register" of her class—may contain an entirely different set of names from her list of November. The total registration of the class may be 75, counting all the aspiring milliners who appeared before her during the term, while her average register may be 40, this being the average length of her roll call with Caroline and Maria coming in January to take the place of Jennie and Marguerite, who dropped out in November; the average attendance may be 24, counting together the number who were present each evening and dividing by the total number of evenings. The per cent of attendance as it is reckoned in the New York evening schools would then be the ratio of 24 to 40, or 60 per cent. Thus estimated for all the schools in 1912–13, with an average register of 49,438 and an average attendance of 34,117, the per cent was 69.

Of the total attendance that year, about 45 per cent were women and girls. The most regular attendance was credited to men over twenty-one years of age, 72 per cent; with girls under twenty-one a close second, 71 per cent; while boys under twenty-one were third, 68 per cent; and women fourth, 67 per cent. These differences obviously are not very great. It should be explained that the poorest attendance was that of the "compulsory boys"; namely, those under sixteen who had left day school before graduating and were required by law to attend evening school. Their attendance record was 60 per cent. They were counted separately from the other boys under twenty-one, who won third place in the percentage of attendance.

A comparison of attendance figures according to subjects studied* showed the best record for classes in English for foreigners, 72 per cent, as compared with 67 per cent in common branches, and 65 per cent in special subjects. The best attendance of all was in the summer classes in English for foreigners, 77 per cent.†

* Ibid., p. 22.

† The first summer evening classes for foreigners in New York were organized on May 2, 1910, in one school building. In 1911, two such schools were in session, and in 1912, four, but in 1913, only three were open because of a shortage in the allowance for evening school instruction.

The attendance ratio also varied according to the specific subject studied, as well as in the main branches of work offered.* Of the subjects in which a hundred or more were registered, the best showing was for embroidery, 69 per cent, and millinery, 69 per cent; and the lowest was electric wiring, 61 per cent. All these figures which have been quoted apply only to evening elementary schools; the differences in high schools are not marked enough to demand discussion.

Briefly stated, then, the terms of the problem are these: An evening school enrolls 1,000 prospective students, the majority of whom apply for admission at the beginning of the school term, while others come in scattered groups at various times through the season. Of these 1,000, 80 never appear in a class room; 920 are marked present in the roll books at least one night. From time to time names are removed from the roll books when night after night they are marked absent. Others are added as they apply. The average length of the roll in all the classes of the school is about 494, and the average attendance only 341 of the possible 1,000 who have come in contact with the school, more or less casually, in the course of the term. This situation is not peculiar to New York. Furthermore, it has persisted through many changes in school administration.

In the report of the evening schools for 1913 attention is wisely turned from a discussion of

* Ibid., p. 26.

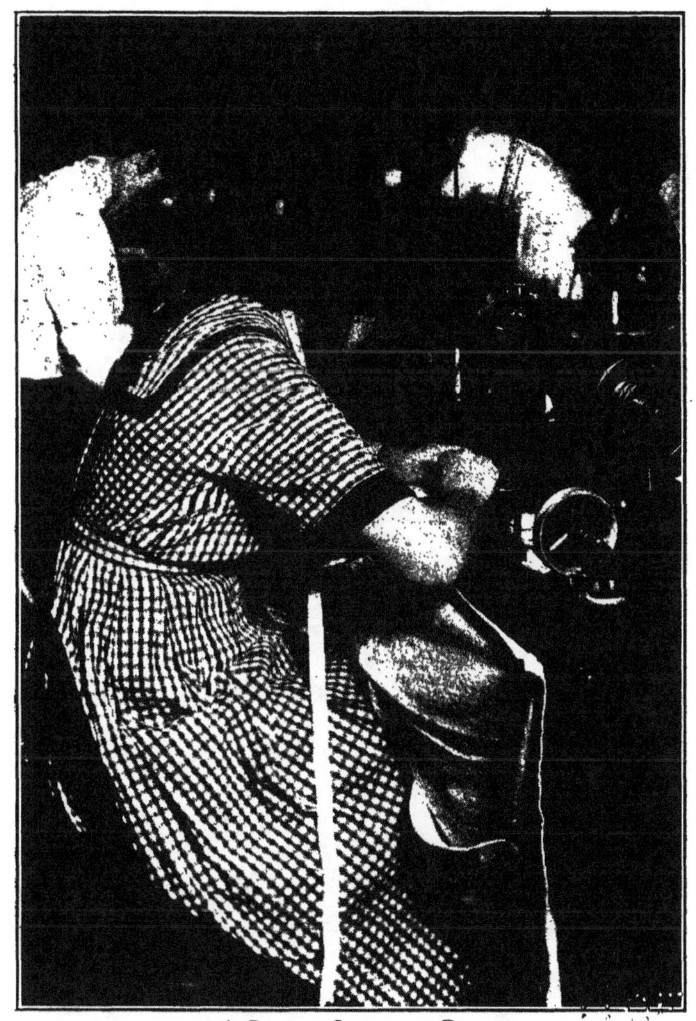

A Button Sewer by Day
Learning machine operating at night

remedies to a realization of the more fundamental implications of this baffling and persistent problem. "Principals might well continue to consider the problem of attendance in their conferences," writes Dr. Shiels,* "not in terms of numbers nor of tenure, but by the indirect and more efficient method of a discussion of the best methods of teaching. It is a great mistake to seek the attendance of pupils on any basis or by any method except the simple and effective one of making school experience so interesting and so valuable that the pupil must realize its worth to him."

The girls included in our investigation were a part of the larger group whose attendance in 1910–11 has been discussed. On the back of each of the investigation cards filled out in the autumn, space was provided for the number of nights the girl was present each month of the school year. As has already been stated, we revisited as late as possible in the spring a majority of the Manhattan and Bronx schools and copied the attendance record of each girl from the teachers' roll books.

Satisfactory data were secured from all† but four of the evening elementary schools included in the investigation in Manhattan, and the records obtained of 2,935 girls out of a total of 3,438 who

* Superintendent of Schools, Fifteenth Annual Report, p. 18.

† The elementary schools from which attendance records were secured were, in Manhattan,—Nos. 4, 13, 14, 17, 19, 23, 29, 38, 45, 59, 67, 71, 72, 89, 92, 93, and 96. Data had been obtained also from schools Nos. 42 and 177, but as so many of the pupils entered late in the term because of Jewish holidays in October, they were omitted on account of this lack of uniformity with results from other schools.

had filled out cards in those schools in the preceding autumn. As the work of transferring these records had to be done before the close of the school term, the last of March, the facts about attendance were secured during March from 13 of the schools, thus carrying the records through February, a period of five months. This was not the full term, however, in those schools. In the remaining four schools the total attendance for the school year, six months, that is, through March, was available through the co-operation of the principals in supplying us with complete lists filled out for us in their offices.

The high schools included in this phase of the study were Morris and Harlem,* two of the four investigated in Manhattan and the Bronx, and records were secured of 1,233 of the 1,336 pupils previously investigated in those schools. The full evening high school term, September through April, was covered.

That we might have a background of information for the attendance facts about our limited group, we secured for the classes in 15 elementary schools† the total actual attendance on the first school night of each month, here shown in Table 26.

On the first night in December the actual number present was higher than on the first night in any

* Facts about attendance in East Side evening high school were secured but not tabulated with those of the other high schools because so many of the pupils had not entered until November, after the Jewish holidays of October.

† Nos. 4, 13, 14, 17, 19, 23, 38, 45, 59, 67, 71, 72, 92, 93, and 96.

TABLE 26.—WOMEN ON REGISTER IN THE YEAR, AND ATTENDANCE ON FIRST SCHOOL NIGHT OF EACH MONTH, IN 15 PUBLIC ELEMENTARY EVENING SCHOOLS

Total number of women on register in year . . 14,722

First school night in month	WOMEN ATTENDING ON THE FIRST SCHOOL NIGHT IN EACH MONTH		
	Number	As a percentage of all women on register in year	As a percentage of the maximum number of women attending on the first school night in any month
October 3, 1910	3,604	24.5	46.4
November 1, 1910	7,491	50.9	96.5
December 1, 1910	7,763	52.7	100.0
January 3, 1911	6,217	42.2	80.1
February 1, 1911	6,719	46.0	86.6
March 1, 1911	5,607	38.0	72.2

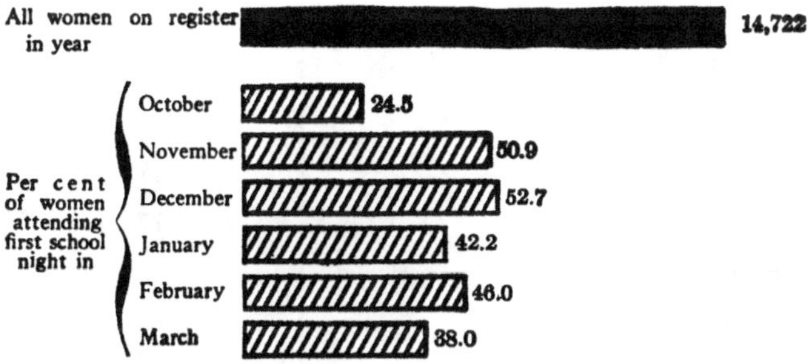

DIAGRAM II.—WOMEN ON REGISTER IN YEAR AND PERCENTAGE ATTENDING FIRST SCHOOL NIGHT OF EACH MONTH, IN 15 PUBLIC ELEMENTARY SCHOOLS

other month of the winter. Taking the number in attendance on the first night in December as the standard, namely, as 100 per cent, the attendance on the first school night in October was only 46 per cent; in March, 72 per cent. Diagram II portrays these same facts graphically. The bad showing in October is due mainly to the fact that so many important Jewish holidays fall just at the opening of the evening school sessions. The Jews are so numerous in the schools that undoubtedly their holidays that month do affect the attendance averages of the whole evening school system.

The total registration* in these 15 evening elemen-

* In the evening high schools, Harlem, Morris, and East Side, we secured the average attendance the first hour each night for two-week periods. In the table which follows, the average for each period is shown as a percentage of the average attendance, for the two weeks ending September 29, 1910:

Period of two weeks ending	Average attendance, as a percentage of average attendance during period ending September 29
September 29	100
October 13	88
27	94
November 10	90
23	94
December 8	84
15	84
January 12	77
26	78
February 9	79
23	81
March 9	80
23	79
April 6	63
27	68
May 16	71

tary schools for the year was 14,722, but the largest number present the first school night of any month was only 7,763, or 53 per cent of the total register. In October it was only 25 per cent with an increase in November to 51 per cent, and, after reaching the December maximum, a fall to 42 per cent in January, a slight increase to 46 per cent in February, and another fall to 38 per cent in March.

These, like the figures quoted from the annual reports of the schools, are composite statistics. To follow the fortunes of the group whom we investigated is to secure a different kind of information, concerning as it does a group of which the personnel did not change in the course of the year. Our first interest was to discover the proportion who were still attending evening school when we returned in the spring. The facts are shown in Table 27, on p. 154.

Of 1,127 evening high school girls investigated who had entered the classes in September, only 477, or 43 per cent, were still attending in May, while 36 per cent had left before the first of January. In the four elementary schools for which information was secured for the full term, 64 per cent stayed through the school year. Stated for the different occupational groups,* the proportion in the manufacturing group continuing until the end of the term was 67 per cent, as compared with 63 per cent among those who had no occupation,

* For attendance by main groups of occupations and ages, see Appendix I, Tables L, M, and N, pp. 209–211.

TABLE 27.—MONTHS IN WHICH WOMEN ATTENDING PUBLIC EVENING SCHOOLS DROPPED OUT[a]

Month	WOMEN DROPPING OUT OF[b]					
	High schools		Elementary schools in which attendance records were secured for			
			Six months		Five months	
	Number	Per cent	Number	Per cent	Number	Per cent
September	46	4	..[d]	..[d]	..[d]	..[d]
October	172	15	88	9	112	6
November	125	11	102	10	254	13
December	67	6	61	6	221	11
January	83	7	77	8	176	9
February	68	6	32	3	..[f]	..[f]
March	54	5	..[e]	..[e]	..[e]	..[e]
April	35	3	..[d]	..[d]	..[d]	..[d]
Women remaining at time attendance records were secured[c]	477	43	613	64	1,230	61
Total	1,127	100	973	100	1,993	100

[a] Data appear in detail in Appendix I, Tables L, M, and N, pp. 209–211.

[b] Data as to month of dropping out were secured for 1,127 of the 4,862 women attending evening high schools, and for 2,966 of the 8,279 women attending evening elementary schools.

[c] Records were secured for the full term for the high schools after they closed in May, and for the full term of four of the elementary schools after they closed in March. Records for 13 elementary schools were secured in March, before the schools closed.

[d] Schools not in session.

[e] Sessions in elementary schools ended in March. As pupils were considered as having dropped out in a given month only when they failed to appear any night in the following month, the numbers dropping out in a given month are stated only when attendance figures were secured for the following month.

[f] Attendance figures were secured only through February, not March.

and 56 per cent in trade and transportation. In the other occupations, the numbers were too few to justify percentages. Grouped by ages, the best showing in these four elementary schools was made by those between the ages of eighteen and twenty-one, of whom 145 of a total of 216, or 67 per cent, continued their course to the end, as compared with 90, or 65 per cent, of the 139 who were twenty-one or over; 158, or 61 per cent, of the 259 under sixteen; and 207, or 60 per cent, of the 343 between sixteen and eighteen.

In the 13 schools for which the data covered five months instead of six, the proportion still enrolled at the end of February was 61 per cent, or 1,230 out of 1,993, varying according to occupational groups from 63 per cent, or 564 out of 890, in manufacturing, and 63 per cent, or 304 out of 483, in trade and transportation, to 59 per cent, or 237 out of 400, in the non-wage-earning group, and 57 per cent, or 123 out of 215, in domestic and personal service. The girls under sixteen here made the best record, 65 per cent, 328 of 501 remaining through February, with 63 per cent, or 379 of the 597, between sixteen and eighteen, 62 per cent, or 255 out of 413, between eighteen and twenty-one, and 58 per cent, or 266 out of 457, twenty-one years of age or older.

Perhaps the most significant fact here is the really insignificant difference between the various groups, whether considered with reference to their occupations or their ages. Efforts to correlate the degree of perseverance in attendance with hours of labor in shop or office brought also negligible results. Undoubtedly the explanation is not that age, occupation, and hours of work are negligible factors, but that each is involved with so many other factors not revealed in the statistics that any attempt to measure their comparative strength by isolating them is foredoomed to failure. For example, the little Bohemian girl of fifteen who leaves the cigar factory at 6 o'clock and walks to her home across the street, finds it less difficult to go to evening school two blocks away than the American high school graduate who leaves a Wall Street office at 5 o'clock and travels home to the Bronx by subway, although the latter probably finds evening school more congenial, and is probably less fatigued by her daily work. Then, too, outside interests and home duties so complicate the situation that we can not measure with accuracy the importance of any single circumstance of work, transit, or evening school methods. The complexity of the situation is well illustrated by the following statements made to us by 86 girls whom we interviewed in their homes to find out why they left evening school.

The kind of information on which this preceding list is based is shown in the following illustrations of the girls' own explanations as we recorded them after our interviews:

"Worked late in December. Also takes music lessons."

TABLE 28.—REASONS GIVEN BY 86 WOMEN FOR LEAVING PUBLIC EVENING SCHOOLS

Reason	Women who left for each specified reason
Reasons connected with daily occupation	
Home late from work	9
Overtime and home work	12
Too tired to go to night school	8
Attending business school	1
Total	30
Family reasons	
Girl's help needed at home	6
Death of relatives	2
Total	8
Personal reasons	
Health poor, night school too confining	9
Poor eyesight	5
Other "attractions"—music lessons, choirs, etc.	9
Could not afford to pay carfare, lived too far from school	3
To go out of town	1
Home too late from school, street not safe	4
Total	31
Reasons connected with school	
"Didn't learn anything"	4
"Didn't care for it"	2
Dissatisfied with school methods	3
Dissatisfied with course	8
Total	17
Grand total	86

"Sister having overtime, and girl couldn't go alone."

"Took the course in hand bookbinding but didn't learn anything and supplies too expensive."

"Ill. Also tired, as she is on her feet all day as a salesgirl. Home late frequently."

"Was put at new machine in bookbinding which made her nervous, and she was so tired when she reached school that she would almost faint."

"Mother afraid to let her go, as there are too many loafers on the street."

"Was taking millinery, but found it would be cheaper to buy hats. Wanted to change to a general course but was told to wait till new term began."

"Did not care for it. School is for 'greenhorns,' and class fools away the time. Might as well stay home and read."

"Too tired at night, and light at school hurt her eyes. Also considers the course too long. Also, has to help mother with the housework."

"Stenographer, works by artificial light by day. Must rest at night."

"Before Christmas worked late and could not attend. Had never been absent before."

"Attended a church fair several evenings and missed the school lessons. Didn't care to return, especially as class was too large (dressmaking) so that she could get very little attention."

"Wanted time for other things."

Regularity of attendance, however, is measured not only by continuance in school until the term is finished, but also by the number of nights a girl is present during the period when she is actually registered. It is pointed out in the New York report on evening schools for 1913 that brief periods of attendance are often legitimate, as when pupils enter trade classes "to learn some particular process, to handle some single machine, to familiarize themselves with some special phases of instruction." The aim accomplished, it is not failure on the part of the school or lack of perseverance in the pupil if the records show only a brief stay. In order to determine the degree of this kind of regularity, the number of evenings attended must be compared with the number of evenings of possible attendance, not throughout the year but through the period of enrollment. This was the method of measuring attendance adopted for our group. As the method of tabulation was somewhat complex it will be described in detail.

The records were grouped first according to schools, then according to ages, with the simple division of those under eighteen and those of eighteen or over, and finally according to the large occupational groups. On the tabulating sheet was recorded for each girl the number of evenings she was present in each month. Regularity of attendance during the year was determined for the different groups of women by combining the percentages of attendance of the women included in each group. Each woman's "percentage of attendance" was the ratio of her actual attendance to her "possible attendance." It was obtained by dividing the number of evenings she was present by the number of school evenings in the months in which she was present at least one evening. If she was present in October and then dropped out until January, school evenings in November and December were not considered in computing her percentage of attendance. "Possible attendance," in other words, equals the number of school evenings in the months in which she was present at least one evening.

The percentage of attendance for a whole year for a group of girls was secured by adding together the individual percentages of attendance, worked out separately for each girl, and then dividing the total by the number of girls in the group. If, for instance, Sophie was present in a high school 16 evenings out of the possible 32 during October and November, and did not appear again, her regularity of attendance was 50 per cent. If Theresa was present at least one evening in each month between September and May and had a total attendance of 90 evenings when the high schools were open 120 evenings in all, her measure of attendance was 75 per cent. If Sophie and Theresa form a group to be studied together, the regularity of attendance of the group is 50 plus 75 divided by 2, or 62.5 per cent.

The percentage of attendance obtained in this way for the period of enrollment was 67 per cent for 1,233 girls in high schools and 71 per cent for 2,935 girls in elementary schools. The classifica-

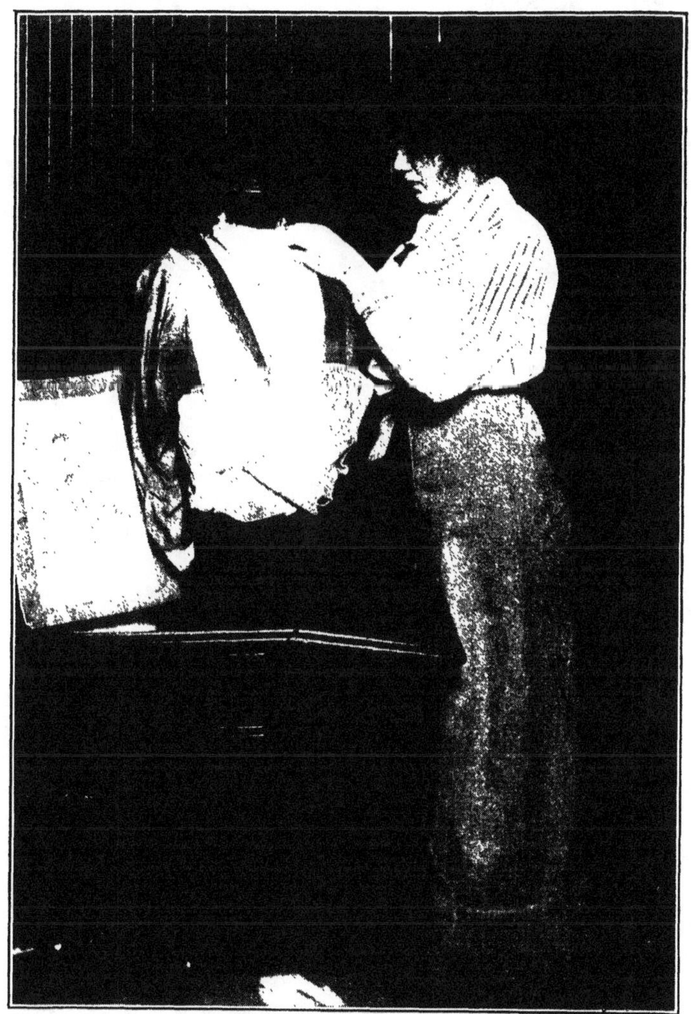

Draping a Chiffon Waist

tion by ages shows a record of 73 per cent during the time of enrollment for girls under eighteen, compared with 68 per cent for girls of eighteen or over. The occupational groups, eliminating professional work, in which the number considered was only four, varied from 64 per cent attendance during the time of enrollment for women in domestic and personal service to 72 per cent in manufacturing and mechanical pursuits, with 69 per cent in trade and transportation and 70 per cent for women who were not at work. The lowest percentage of attendance during the period of enrollment for any one school was 56, and the highest, 88.

Irregularity of attendance means a waste of school equipment and time. It means that the schools accomplish less than they seem to accomplish. The evening schools are in session, comparatively speaking, but a few evenings in each month, and where attendance is irregular the average number of evenings of instruction per pupil may be considerably lower than the number of evenings the schools are in session. The average number of evenings of attendance per woman during a month was obtained by dividing the total number of evenings of actual attendance in the month by the number of women who were present at least one evening. To take a simple illustration, the schools were in session nine evenings during the month of December, 1910. Assuming that, of a group of nine girls, only two attended every evening, while five attended seven evenings, one attended two evenings, and one attended one evening, we find that the total attendance of the group was 56 evenings. Dividing 56 by the number of girls in the group, 9, we have an average attendance of 6.2 evenings. The results of our computations are presented in Table 29, and graphically portrayed in Diagram III.

The table shows that the school facilities were actually used in each month fewer evenings than the schools were in session. Thus in October, when the schools were in session 16 evenings, the average number of evenings attended both in high schools and in elementary schools was but 11 evenings; and in March, when the schools were in session 18 evenings, the average number of evenings attended was but 13.

The reasons for irregularity of attendance are undoubtedly similar to those already discussed as the cause of dropping out before the close of the term. Those statements grouped themselves naturally under certain main heads, with, of course, many subsidiary circumstances in individual cases,—reasons connected with school and the failure of teachers to hold the interest of the pupils, reasons connected with work, conditions at home, personal reasons and outside interests. Undoubtedly attendance will be improved as methods of teaching in the evening schools grow more efficient, but even then, if the facts which we have discussed are safe bases for prophecy, 100 per cent of the pupils will not attend 100 per cent of the time. For, as we have pointed out in the beginning of the chapter, the biggest handicap in evening school

TABLE 29.—EVENINGS IN WHICH SCHOOLS WERE IN SESSION EACH MONTH, AND AVERAGE NUMBER OF EVENINGS OF ATTENDANCE PER WOMAN, FOR 1,233 WOMEN ATTENDING EVENING HIGH SCHOOLS AND 2,935 WOMEN ATTENDING EVENING ELEMENTARY SCHOOLS[a]

Month	EVENING HIGH SCHOOLS		EVENING ELEMENTARY SCHOOLS	
	School evenings in month	Average evenings of attendance in month per woman	School evenings in month	Average evenings of attendance in month per woman
September	8	6.8	..[b]	..[b]
October	16	11.0	16	10.9
November	16	11.8	16	12.0
December	9	6.9	9	7.1
January	17	12.1	17	12.5
February	14	10.1	14	10.7
March	18	13.0	18	13.4
April	12	8.9	..[b]	..[b]
May	10	8.7	..[b]	..[b]

[a] Complete attendance figures were secured for 1,233 of the 4,862 women attending evening high schools, and for 2,935 of the 8,279 women attending evening elementary schools.

[b] Elementary schools not in session.

work is the fact that it must be done in the evening. It is the bearing of this fact on a program of industrial education which is of importance from

EVENING HIGH SCHOOLS

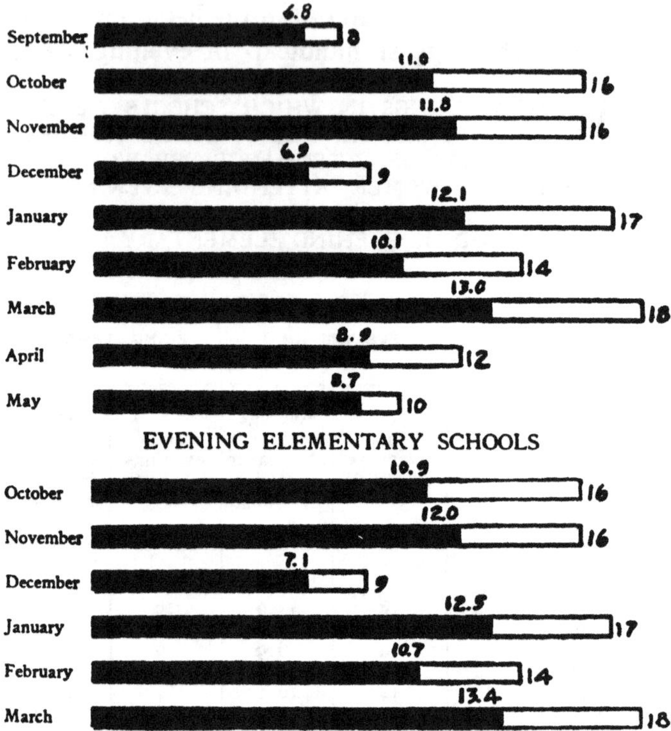

The total length of each bar represents the number of evenings the schools were in session, and the shaded portion represents average evenings of attendance per woman.

DIAGRAM III.—EVENINGS IN WHICH SCHOOLS WERE IN SESSION EACH MONTH, AND AVERAGE NUMBER OF EVENINGS OF ATTENDANCE PER WOMAN FOR 1,233 WOMEN ATTENDING EVENING HIGH SCHOOLS AND 2,935 WOMEN ATTENDING EVENING ELEMENTARY SCHOOLS

the point of view of our investigation, rather than any specific recommendations which we might be able to make to the schools.

First, the facts seem to us to show conclusively that if a system of compulsory continuation schools for young wage-earners is to be developed, their sessions must be held by day and not by night. The present law requiring boys under sixteen who have not yet graduated from grammar school to attend evening school is a refined form of cruelty. Even grown men and women, however ambitious they may be, find it difficult to persevere in a night class, and to compel young boys to carry such a burden is inconsistent with all our efforts to do away with child labor. Furthermore, it is a farce. No attendance officers are assigned to bring in the boys and only a minority ever appear in the evening schools. Those who come attend more irregularly than any other group. The law of 1913 which gave boards of education throughout the state the power to compel boys and girls under sixteen to attend part-time schools between the hours o 8 a.m. and 5 p.m., is a long step forward.

Second, as a corollary of this recommendation that continuation schooling for young wage-earners should be given by day and not at night, it would seem desirable to exclude from evening schools all boys and girls under sixteen. The information which we have secured showing that of the girls under sixteen investigated by us, one in three reported no occupation to prevent her attending day school, is an indication that the evening schools may be quite unconsciously making it easier for girls of this age to leave day school. They like the excitement and the grown-up feeling of going to school at night. On the other hand, it is a fact recognized in many reports of evening schools that the presence of young boys and girls is often an embarrassment and a hindrance to older pupils who are eager to make good the deficiencies in their training. Years ago it was the twelve-year-olds and even the eight-year-olds whose exclusion was recommended. We might now take a step forward and definitely set apart the evening schools for those who are at least sixteen years old. Perhaps it would be one step toward keeping children out of industry until they are sixteen.

Third, with the problem of the children eliminated, the schools could be more readily adapted to the needs of the older pupils. It is beyond the scope of this chapter to outline a program for such adaptation,* but one fact stands out clearly from a consideration of the attendance problem and the difficulties which it reveals in the path of aspiring students. The schools are now open in the winter months, from October to March or April in the elementary classes, with a month more added at each end in the high schools. It is a well-known fact that these are the busy months in many industries, while the cold weather and the early nightfall make evening school attendance

* Those who are interested in the development of evening schools will find an able discussion of the subject in its many phases in Dr. Albert Shiels' Reports on Evening Schools for the Years Ending July 31, 1912 and 1913, Fourteenth and Fifteenth Annual Reports of the Superintendent of Schools, New York City.

exceedingly difficult. Recently summer sessions have been organized to teach English to foreigners and the attendance has been more regular than in the winter term. Thousands of working men and women are much less overworked and overstrained in the summer months. It would be an interesting experiment to offer them the opportunity to join evening classes from April to October. More important than this specific suggestion, however, is the principle underlying it,—to adapt the evening schools more and more perfectly to conditions in the lives of wage-earners, to offer them what they need when they need it, and at seasons when they are able to take full advantage of it.

CHAPTER VII

SOME PROBLEMS OF INDUSTRIAL EDUCATION

THESE thirteen thousand girls whose school careers and subsequent occupations have been reviewed in the preceding chapters have proved by the fact of their attendance at night school that they desired, more or less vaguely, some additional education. In many instances their enrollment in a night class was a protest against inadequate schooling in early years and inadequate training in shop or factory since their wage-earning began. Whether the failure of the school was due to lack of vocational training during the years they could attend, these workers could not have told us definitely or conclusively; but neither could many famous educators reach a definite conclusion even with all the facts before them. For of all the problems of school or industry today, perhaps none is more baffling than the one which is common to both, namely, that of industrial education.

It is generally conceded that if the problem of industrial training be a difficult one for boys, it is still more so for girls. For boys, wage-earning is considered a matter of course, but that the complexity of our economic life requires wage-earning of girls also—as is becoming increasingly the case —the public does not yet realize. To know the facts about these thirteen thousand girls in evening school is to advance a little way, therefore, toward an understanding of economic conditions and a comprehension of some of the most difficult and baffling problems in current educational and industrial policy. Changing conditions of industry; variety and range of occupations; monotony, long hours, and specialized tasks; evidences of exploitation of workers; an early beginning of the wage-earning career, and consequently, a short period for schooling,—these are the salient conditions brought out in this study.

Successive reports of the evening schools have discussed the rapid changes in women's work. Slightly more than fifty years ago the sewing machine had been recently introduced and the development of the department store was just beginning. Employment of women in stores was advocated by the board of education to relieve the unfortunate condition in the sewing trades resulting from the displacement of hand workers through the introduction of the sewing machine. The process of change has brought about a rapid development of new tasks through increasing complexity in industrial life. Those who advocate confining the vocational training of women to the traditional home pursuits, such as sewing and cooking, do not take into account the fact that the work of girls outside the home is now an established factor in industrial life. Interesting testimony on this point was offered recently by a group of women well qualified to speak; namely, by the delegates at the fourth biennial convention of the National Women's Trade Union League. The president, in discussing industrial education, declared that "no denial of trade education will keep a girl out of a trade, and if she is denied entrance by the front door as a skilled, trained artisan, she will enter by the back door as an under-bidder." *

The evening school girls included in this study were employed in manufacturing and mechanical pursuits, in trade and transportation, in professions, and in domestic and personal service. The occupations of the girls employed in manufacturing and mechanical pursuits are illustrative of the many subdivisions within these large industrial groups. In the manufacture of diverse products, these girls were at work in nine large industries, with 82 distinct trade divisions and a countless number of processes of work within these divisions. The New York state department of labor lists 12 large industrial groups in this state, and all but three of them—the manufacture of paper and pulp, the building trades, and the industry of supplying water, light, and power in cities and villages—were

* *Life and Labor*, August, 1913, p. 231. Published monthly by the National Women's Trade Union League, Chicago.

represented on the record cards of the evening school girls.

"Entering by the back door as an under-bidder" seems to have been the lot of many women workers, if the results of recent investigations are to be credited. Educators must take into consideration not only the variety and range of women's tasks, but the conditions which are deplorable in industry today. For, to train boys and girls for work which stunts and injures them, would be a new form of exploitation. Factory management must create conditions in harmony with the ideal of the educator, which is to secure a fuller life for men and women. The community must ask this question before planning a program of industrial education: Are employers of labor ready to meet their full share of responsibility by changing the conditions which are now producing inefficiency and checking mental development? Monotony in work, long hours of employment, and child labor are indicative of the conditions which need changing.

Consider as an example of monotonous work one of the pictures given us in the United States government report on woman wage-earners:

"The catcher (in a cigarette factory) sits before the cigarette machine, catching the cigarettes as they fall, stacking them on the trays, and examining them for imperfections. The work requires some training, as the catcher must be able to tell at a glance whether the cigarette is too soft, or too hard, whether it is crumpled at the end, or shows any other imperfection. She sits at her work and has no opportunity for a change of position unless the machine is stopped to make some adjustment. During a day of ten hours the catcher will catch and examine from 130,000 to 200,000 cigarettes."*

Or again: Hand packing

"also is a woman's occupation. The packer sits at a long bench on which are the cartons and the trays of cigarettes brought from the machines. Aligning the cigarettes on the bench in front of them, the packers rapidly push or place them in the box, usually handling five at a time, and close the box. The work is light and easy and the only strain involved is that due to the demand for speed. The movements soon become mechanical, so that the packer is apt to keep her hands and body moving unconsciously even when she is not packing."†

Pasting internal revenue stamps upon packages of cigarettes is another process which so captures the worker, body and soul, that movement becomes as involuntary as the throb of machinery.

"Taking a row of stamps in her right hand and a package of cigarettes in her left, the woman puts a stamp over the end, gives a quick jerk which tears it off from the row, puts the package back, seizes another, repeats the operation, and so on indefinitely. The women and girls get to doing his sort of work very

* Report on Condition of Woman and Child Wage-Earners in the United States. Vol. XVIII, Employment of Women and Children in Selected Industries, p. 81. U. S. Senate Document No. 645.

† Ibid., p. 83.

rapidly, as it is wholly mechanical. Some of them fall into a rhythmic jerking of the hand and swinging of the body which they keep up even when halted for a short time by some lack of material."*

Vivid illustrations these, of a kind of skill which makes no demand upon the intelligence, while it adapts the body perfectly to its own purposes. Such tasks have a more serious effect upon the physical and mental condition when hours of labor are prolonged. That working hours are too long is shown by the reports of girls in the evening schools. In manufacturing, only 15 per cent were working eight hours or less; in stores, only 4.5 per cent worked eight hours or less, while 52 per cent worked between eight and nine hours a day, 36 per cent between nine and nine and one-half, and 7.5 per cent, nine and one-half or longer. Eighty-four of every 100 of the factory girls began work before 8:30 a.m. and only 19 in every 100 stopped work before half-past five. Over half of the factory workers, 51 per cent, and 41 per cent in trade and transportation, did not leave work until 6 o'clock or later. These were the normal hours, and in the busy season they were often prolonged.

Long hours of work were not confined to older workers. Even the fourteen- and fifteen-year-old children were subject to them, although often in violation of the state law. Only 16 per cent, or 104

* Ibid., p. 83.

of 665 girls under sixteen in trade and transportation, worked less than eight hours daily, and 16 per cent had an eight-hour day, while 41 per cent worked between eight and nine hours, and 27 per cent nine hours or longer. In factories, 592 of 898 factory girls under sixteen, or 66 per cent, were working longer than eight hours, in spite of the fact that eight hours is the legal limit for children under sixteen in manufacturing establishments.

That these children should be attending evening school at all after such hours is deplorable. Indeed, many believe now that their presence in industrial establishments is a reproach to industry and the community. So long as we permit girls and boys to go to work at the age of fourteen, we must expect the wage-earners of the future to suffer not only from the bad effects of premature employment, but from inadequate schooling.

Of 10,676 of the evening school girls of all ages whose reports of their school careers showed the age when they left school, 40 per cent left at the age of fourteen and 14 per cent were even younger than fourteen. Only 20 per cent had stayed until they were sixteen or older.

To leave school to go to work at an early age is one of the signs of an inadequate standard of living in the community—interpreting standard of living to mean not only food, clothing, and housing, but educational ideals—and is due to as great a

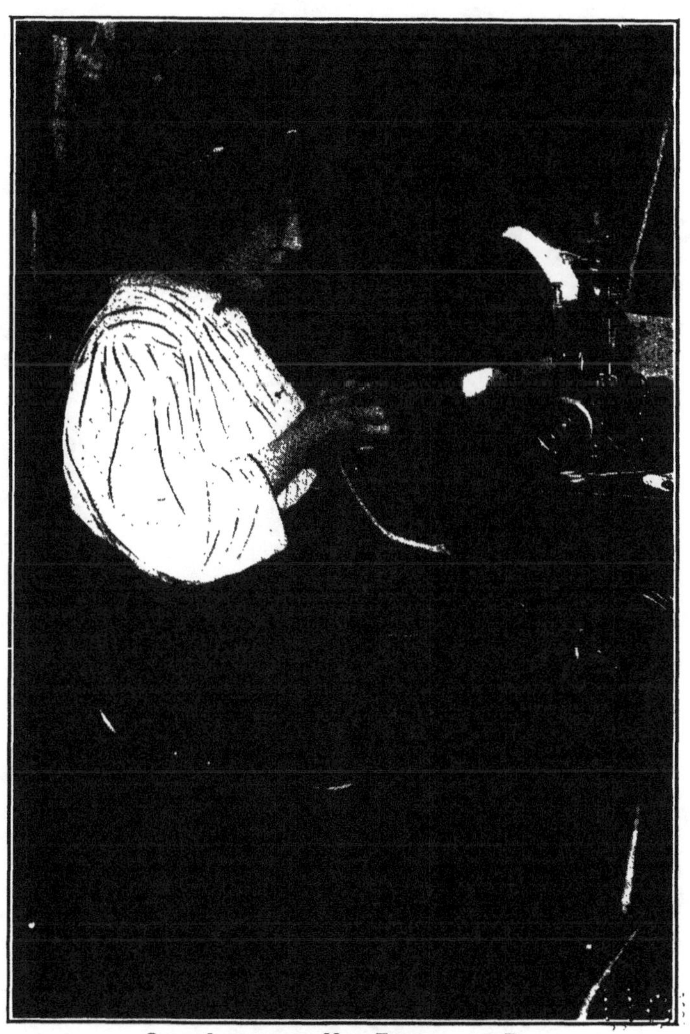

Sews Linings in Hat Factory by Day
Learning to make the hats at night

variety of causes as determine standards of living. Of the evening school girls who were asked why they had left school before the age of sixteen, exactly half reported that their earnings had been necessary at home, and their statements were corroborated by their families. Only seven of another group of 180 working girls under sixteen lived with relatives who were not members of their immediate family, while the others, 101, were living in their own homes, and the fathers of more than three-fourths of these, 77, were at work. Undoubtedly these families did feel economic pressure, due probably to inadequate wages earned by the father.

Thus it is that the problem of industrial education in this manifestation of it, namely, the early termination of the school career, is closely related to the conditions which produce poverty in the community. On the other hand, it may have been questionable whether the poverty of these families was relieved to any appreciable extent by the employment of their children for low wages, often in irregular work, without any foundation training for future earning capacity. The community can do much to remedy this condition directly by prolonging the years of schooling for children. Already an apparently simple and unimportant change in the compulsory education law and the labor law, requiring that a child complete the sixth grade instead of merely reaching the fifth grade, as heretofore, before he is able to secure a work certificate, has resulted in cutting down the issuance of work certificates; * and that, too, in a year in which unemployment had been a serious problem and economic pressure in wage-earners' families in New York unusually severe.

That the length of attendance in school and the grade reached does bear some relation to the later choice of an occupation, is revealed by a study of the facts among 10,000 of these evening school pupils. Only 33 per cent of the group had had nine years or more of schooling; but this proportion varied from 23 per cent in manufacturing and 24 per cent in domestic and personal service to 38 per cent in trade and transportation and 81 per cent in the professions.

Over 8,000 girls reported that the last school attended was a public school in New York City. Of the girls in this group, for whom data as to grade at leaving school were available, 40 in every 100 left before graduating from an elementary school, 37 per cent graduated but did not continue to high school, 23 per cent entered high school, but only 3 per cent finished the high school course. It is significant, however, that in professional service 72 per cent were high school graduates, as compared

* The number of employment certificates issued in the first quarter of 1914, compared with the corresponding period in 1913, in New York City, is as follows:

1913	10,418
1914	7,800

(These figures are furnished by the department of health. They are not yet in print elsewhere.)

with the small fraction of 1 per cent (.2 per cent) of those employed in manufacturing. Of the factory girls, 55 per cent reached the fifth, sixth, or seventh grades in the elementary school. In trade and transportation, the proportion who finished the elementary grades was comparatively large, 76 per cent as compared with 31 per cent of the factory girls. Some one of the tasks offered in manufacturing or mechanical pursuits, or in domestic or personal service, would appear to offer the most common opportunity for the child who leaves elementary school before graduating. If she reaches graduation day she is more likely to find work in some branch of trade and transportation, and if she completes the high school course she may ultimately become a professional worker.

For the large majority of workers in factory industries, according to our statistics, the schools under present conditions must complete their task of training in less than nine years. Within the manufacturing group, the facts regarding grade reached in school vary greatly for the different trades. A rough comparison with census figures regarding wages seems to indicate that the girls whose progress in school, measured by grades covered, was cut short, were most likely to enter the lowest-paid occupations. In brief, there would appear to be a great difference in different trades in requiring from workers the kind of foundation training now offered in the schools; or perhaps it is fundamentally a difference in the amount of intelligence required,—a difference showing first in school progress and later in occupational efficiency. Only a detailed study of conditions within these occupations could show in a more fundamental way the real significance of this situation, if, indeed, we are justified in drawing a conclusion from the data at hand.

The school authorities in New York are keenly alive to the need for trade education, although the term "trade education" has, as yet, only a vague meaning. In the last report of the president of the board of education, issued in January, 1914, this statement is made:*

"We are not, in this city, doing nearly enough along the lines of vocational education. Something more is needed than the mere writing of reports upon the needs. Over 40,000 young boys and girls leave our elementary schools annually to go to work. Only a very small proportion of our elementary school graduates go on into high school. Our trade schools have an enrollment of only 857—a pitiably small number in proportion to the numbers leaving the school system to go to work. No other problem of education is of more concern to the board of education than this . . . .

"In favor of continuation instruction for wage-earners, there is absolute agreement. Hitherto, this continuation work in the schools of this city has, with slight exception, been carried on in the evening schools, and the development of industrial instruction in these

* Board of Education, New York City. Report of the President, January, 1914, p. 9.

schools within the last two years has been a considerable one. It is desirable, however, that continuation classes should be established during the day. Under such conditions pupils will receive instruction during working hours and not after a day of exhausting labor."

By a state law, to which reference has already been made,* boards of education in the various cities who may decide to organize part-time classes by day are given legislative authority to compel the attendance of girls and boys under sixteen. This leaves the way open for experiment along this line. Meanwhile, evening classes for wage-earners, like those already described in Chapter V, are making valuable experiments. The Manhattan Trade School for Girls and the Vocational School for Boys represent a different type of industrial education from that given in these evening or continuation classes; namely, preliminary practice in specific trade processes. Thus far, however, as the statement just quoted shows, this kind of preliminary trade training has been accessible to only a very small number of students. Whether or not it will prove desirable to extend it can be decided only by a thorough testing of results already achieved.

The following are some of the questions which have not yet been answered conclusively in any community: Is industrial education to be chiefly practice in processes of work as training for a specific trade, or will it prove possible to discover

* See footnote, p. 74.

certain fundamental principles common to many industries, which can be made part of the school curriculum and which will train children in general efficiency as a foundation for later training in industry? What shall be done for the workers whose special tasks require no practice except that which can readily be secured in a workroom and whose occupations involve no fundamental principles? Consider, for example, the evening school girl whose sole occupation was to put nuts on cakes and whose previous work had been to paste chenille dots on veils. If it is desirable to extend the work of trade schools which give specific, preliminary training for industries, is it within the bounds of possibility that the New York schools should some day be able to give such training in the processes of every occupation in the community? If a community must select the occupations for which courses will be offered, what shall be the basis of selection? To what extent will increased efficiency in the teaching force and an improved curriculum in the elementary school result in so strengthening the foundation training that some of the later problems of industrial education will disappear? If the age limit for employment be raised to sixteen years, what types of courses shall be offered to children between the ages of fourteen and sixteen? If the continuation schools now advocated by the New York board of education should be established, how can the courses be planned so that they shall not be echoes of elementary teaching but adapted to the needs of young workers in a great variety of occupations?

These are puzzling questions, relating not only to the evening schools but to the whole educational system. The fact that they are being asked in so many communities and answered experimentally is hopeful.

The development of industrial education, however, depends not only upon the schools but also upon modern industry. The methods of training workers must change with changing requirements in the shops. It is an open question as to whether the process of specialization will be carried further, whether more and more machinery will be introduced until production shall have become chiefly automatic, or whether there will be an increasing opportunity for individual skill. It is the need for individual skill which the schools can most readily meet. Far more difficult is the problem of broadening the outlook of workers employed in monotonous unskilled tasks.

The movement for raising the standards in industry through legislation will undoubtedly be an important factor in bringing about changed conditions. Hours are being reduced, the employment of children discouraged, and even rates of pay regulated by the community. Already nine states* have passed minimum wage laws, eight of

* Brief on Behalf of Respondents; Stettler *vs.* Industrial Welfare Commission of the State of Oregon. Supreme Court of the State of Oregon, October Term, 1913; p. 3, Insert.

which provide for commissions to determine rates of pay for each industry, and one establishes by law a definite minimum wage. Other states, New York among them, have appointed commissions to study wages. The raising of wages may tend to make the employment of inefficient and unskilled workers for minor tasks and odd jobs too expensive, and may compel employers to pay more attention both to the training of employes and to the reorganization of work.

It is because of these increasingly important influences in the conduct of business, as well as because of the inevitable changes in industrial methods which grow out of new inventions and new ideas of management, that industrial education becomes for the schools a problem to be solved only by searching inquiry, by experiment, and by constant readjustment to changing conditions.

NOTES ON CENSUS OF OCCUPATIONS, 1910

As this book goes to press, the volume on occupations in 1910 is just received from the bureau of the census. The total number* of women gainfully employed in New York City in 1910 was 586,193, as compared with 367,437 in 1900. The increase was larger than the increase in number of women in the population. In 1900, of every 100 women ten years of age and over in the city, 27 were gainfully employed, while in 1910, 31 in every hundred were at work. The number employed in manufacturing and mechanical pursuits was 207,959, or 35.5 per cent of the whole group of wage-earning women, in trade and transportation 137,778 or 23.5 per cent, in domestic and personal service, 191,152 or 32.6 per cent, and in professional service 48,423 or 8.3 per cent. Comparison with the chart on page 53 shows that the proportion in trade and transportation had increased from 17.8 per cent to 23.5 per cent, while the group in manufacturing and mechanical pursuits was 35.5 per cent of the total as compared with 36.1 per cent in 1900. The proportion in professional service increased slightly, while domestic and personal service decreased from 39.9 per cent to 32.6 per cent. Of all the wage-earners in the city—2,152,433—the men numbered 1,566,240, and the women 586,193, or 27 per cent as compared with 25 per cent in 1900.

* Thirteenth United States Census, 1910. Occupation Statistics, p. 180

APPENDICES

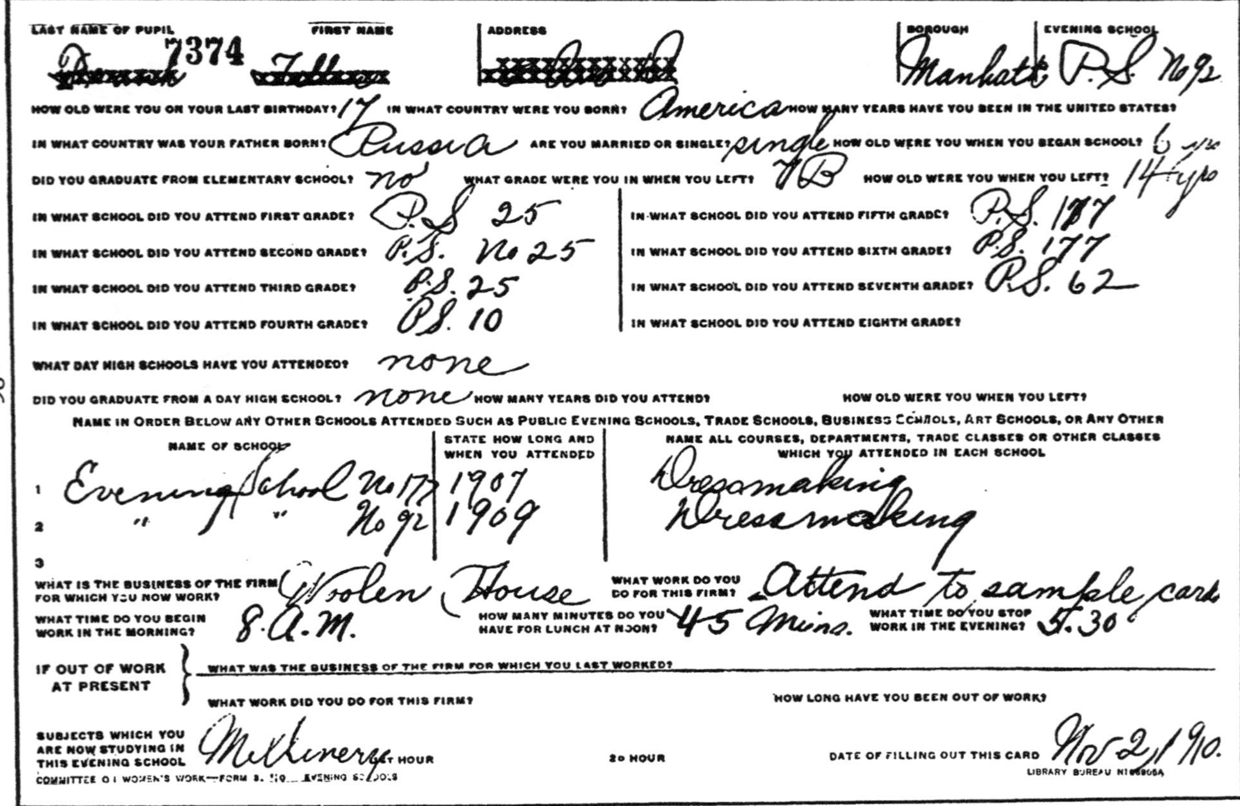

LAST NAME OF PUPIL 7374 FIRST NAME ADDRESS BOROUGH Manhatt EVENING SCHOOL P.S. No 92

HOW OLD WERE YOU ON YOUR LAST BIRTHDAY? 17 IN WHAT COUNTRY WERE YOU BORN? America HOW MANY YEARS HAVE YOU BEEN IN THE UNITED STATES?

IN WHAT COUNTRY WAS YOUR FATHER BORN? Russia ARE YOU MARRIED OR SINGLE? single HOW OLD WERE YOU WHEN YOU BEGAN SCHOOL? 6 yrs

DID YOU GRADUATE FROM ELEMENTARY SCHOOL? no WHAT GRADE WERE YOU IN WHEN YOU LEFT? 7B HOW OLD WERE YOU WHEN YOU LEFT? 14 yrs

IN WHAT SCHOOL DID YOU ATTEND FIRST GRADE?	P.S. 25	IN WHAT SCHOOL DID YOU ATTEND FIFTH GRADE?	P.S. 177
IN WHAT SCHOOL DID YOU ATTEND SECOND GRADE?	P.S. No 25	IN WHAT SCHOOL DID YOU ATTEND SIXTH GRADE?	P.S. 177
IN WHAT SCHOOL DID YOU ATTEND THIRD GRADE?	P.S. 25	IN WHAT SCHOOL DID YOU ATTEND SEVENTH GRADE?	P.S. 62
IN WHAT SCHOOL DID YOU ATTEND FOURTH GRADE?	P.S. 10	IN WHAT SCHOOL DID YOU ATTEND EIGHTH GRADE?	

WHAT DAY HIGH SCHOOLS HAVE YOU ATTENDED? none

DID YOU GRADUATE FROM A DAY HIGH SCHOOL? none HOW MANY YEARS DID YOU ATTEND? HOW OLD WERE YOU WHEN YOU LEFT?

NAME IN ORDER BELOW ANY OTHER SCHOOLS ATTENDED SUCH AS PUBLIC EVENING SCHOOLS, TRADE SCHOOLS, BUSINESS SCHOOLS, ART SCHOOLS, OR ANY OTHER

	NAME OF SCHOOL	STATE HOW LONG AND WHEN YOU ATTENDED	NAME ALL COURSES, DEPARTMENTS, TRADE CLASSES OR OTHER CLASSES WHICH YOU ATTENDED IN EACH SCHOOL
1	Evening School No 177	1907	Dressmaking
2	" " No 92	1909	Dressmaking
3			

WHAT IS THE BUSINESS OF THE FIRM FOR WHICH YOU NOW WORK? Woolen House WHAT WORK DO YOU DO FOR THIS FIRM? Attend to sample cards

WHAT TIME DO YOU BEGIN WORK IN THE MORNING? 8 A.M. HOW MANY MINUTES DO YOU HAVE FOR LUNCH AT NOON? 45 Mins. WHAT TIME DO YOU STOP WORK IN THE EVENING? 5.30

IF OUT OF WORK AT PRESENT { WHAT WAS THE BUSINESS OF THE FIRM FOR WHICH YOU LAST WORKED? WHAT WORK DID YOU DO FOR THIS FIRM? HOW LONG HAVE YOU BEEN OUT OF WORK?

SUBJECTS WHICH YOU ARE NOW STUDYING IN THIS EVENING SCHOOL Millinery 1st HOUR 2nd HOUR DATE OF FILLING OUT THIS CARD Nov 2, 1910.

COMMITTEE ON WOMEN'S WORK—FORM 3. NO.... EVENING SCHOOLS LIBRARY BUREAU N1069064

APPENDIX I

TABLES

TABLE A.[a]—WOMEN ATTENDING PUBLIC EVENING SCHOOLS, WHO WERE INCLUDED IN THIS INVESTIGATION, AND WOMEN FOR WHOM INFORMATION IS PRESENTED IN THE DIFFERENT TABLES[a]

Number of table and subject	Women to whom subject of table applied	Women who supplied information	Women who did not supply information
1. Women who filled record cards for this investigation . .	13,141	13,141	.....
2. Nativity of women . . .	13,141	13,050	91
3. Nativity of fathers of women .	13,141	12,768	373
4. Ages of women	13,141	12,987	154
6. Daily occupations . . .	13,141	13,141	.....
7. Main groups of occupations in manufacturing and mechanical pursuits	4,519	4,519	.....
8. Daily occupations of women employed in trade and transportation	4,505	4,505	.....
10. Normal daily hours of work in manufacturing and mechanical pursuits, and in trade and transportation	9,024	7,516	1,508[b]
11. Hours of beginning and leaving work in manufacturing and mechanical pursuits, and in trade and transportation:			
Hours of beginning work .	9,024	7,671	1,353[b]
Hours of leaving work . .	9,024	7,674	1,350[b]
12. Normal daily hours of work of girls under sixteen years of age employed in trade and transportation	740	665	75[c]
13. Normal daily hours of work of girls under sixteen years of age employed in manufacturing and mechanical pursuits . .	1,044	898	146[d]
14. Day schools previously attended at any time by women attending evening schools . . .	13,141	11,745	1,396[e]
15. Last day school attended . .	13,141	12,276	865

[a] Table continued on following pages. See footnotes, p. 189.

TABLE A (Continued)

Number of table and subject	Women to whom subject of table applied	Women who supplied information	Women who did not supply information
16. Proportion of women whose only previous day school attendance was in New York public schools	13,141	11,745	1,396[e]
17. Grade at leaving school of women who last attended day school in a New York public school .	8,174	7,854	320
18. Grade at leaving school of women who last attended day school in a New York public school, and employed in five selected manufacturing pursuits . .	755	706	49
19. Progress made in elementary school by women who had attended New York public schools only	6,520	5,711	809
20. Years of attendance at day school	13,141	10,119	3,022[e]
21. Age at leaving school . . .	13,141	10,676	2,465[e]
27. Months in which women attending public evening schools dropped out	13,141	4,093	9,048
B. Women who filled record cards, by schools	13,141	13,141	......
C. Nativity of fathers of women, by schools	13,141	12,768	373
D. Industries of women employed in manufacturing and mechanical pursuits, by type of school and borough	4,519	4,519	......
E. Length of noon recess in manufacturing and mechanical pursuits and in trade and transportation	9,024	7,629	1,395[b]
F. Normal daily hours of work of women employed in manufacturing and mechanical pursuits, by main groups of occupations	4,519	3,470	1,049[f]
G. Ages of women by principal occupational groups and by selected occupations . . .	13,141	12,987	154

TABLE A (Continued)

Number of table and subject	Women to whom subject of table applied	Women who supplied information	Women who did not supply information
H. Age at leaving school of women employed in manufacturing and mechanical pursuits, by main groups of occupations .	4,519	3,088	1,431[g]
I. Years of attendance at high school of women who last attended day school in New York public high schools . .	1,803	1,741	62
J. Women in selected occupations in trade and transportation and in manufacturing and mechanical pursuits by			
Age	6,494	6,429	65
Nativity of fathers . .	6,494	6,298	196
Nativity of women . .	6,494	6,447	47
Last school attended . .	6,494	6,049	445
Age at leaving school . .	6,494	5,187	1,307
Daily hours of work . .	6,494	5,433	1,061
K. Grade at leaving school for women who last attended day school in a New York public school, in manufacturing and mechanical pursuits by			
Principal occupations . .	2,212	2,027	185
Selected occupations . .	4,127	4,034	93

[a] Tables 5, 9, 22, 26, and 28, and Tables L, M, and N are omitted because they are not adapted to this table. See tables.

[b] Including 511 unemployed or working at home, and 680 who were in an evening school for which the data as to hours were found to be inaccurate and were not tabulated.

[c] Including 44 unemployed and 10 who were in an evening school for which the data as to hours were found to be inaccurate and were not tabulated.

[d] Including 59 unemployed and 58 in an evening school for which the data as to hours were found to be inaccurate and were not tabulated.

[e] Including 896 in evening schools for which data on the location of day schools attended were incomplete and were not tabulated.

[f] Including 193 unemployed or working at home, and 658 who were in an evening school for which the data as to hours were found to be inaccurate and were not tabulated.

[g] Including 827 in two schools for which the data on age at leaving day school were incomplete and were not tabulated.

TABLE B.*—PUBLIC EVENING SCHOOLS INCLUDED IN THE INVESTIGATION, REGISTRATION, AND AVERAGE ATTENDANCE OF WOMEN IN THESE SCHOOLS DURING THE REGULAR TERM, AND NUMBER OF WOMEN FOR WHOM RECORDS WERE TABULATED BY LOCATION AND TYPE OF SCHOOL

Location and designation of school	Register of women	Average attendance of women	Women included in the investigation
MANHATTAN AND THE BRONX			
High and trade schools:			
East Side high	1,199	687	847
Harlem high	2,088	781	883
Morris high, mixed	1,220[a]	398	453
New York high and trade	1,269	464	404
Total	5,776	2,330	2,587
Elementary schools			
4	1,126	524	161
10	698	230	443
13	1,192	565	143
14	538	188	179
17	500	268	333
19	1,223	382	113
23	245	145	135
29	302	90	44
38	400	228	136
42	1,605	698	717
45	677	227	247
59	626	253	250
67	778	291	111
71	1,725	702	212
72	2,425	718	405
89	507	205	114
92	1,347	440	109
93	644	270	228
96	1,079	561	518
157	755	386	282
177	996	362	179
Total	19,388	7,733	5,059
BROOKLYN AND LONG ISLAND CITY			
High and trade schools:			
Bay Ridge high	562	165	139
Brooklyn trade, mixed	460[b]	175	228
Central high	1,592	636	1,029
Long Island City high and trade, mixed	449[a]	131	188
Williamsburg high	1,071	492	691
Total	4,134	1,599	2,275

* Table continued on following page. See footnotes, p. 191.

TABLE B (Continued)

Location and type of school	Register of women	Average attendance of women	Women included in the investigation
BROOKLYN AND LONG ISLAND CITY			
Elementary schools			
2	678	255	285
5	539	158	167
15	907	476	444
18	728	306	187
22	688	248	255
26	577	257	219
40	351	131	180
92	195	73	57
101	150	52	52
103	137	62	42
134	214	60	33
141	1,142	514	258
142	556	234	164
144	561	166	54
145	716	320	241
150	821	333	182
157	445	191	194
158	539	167	206
Total	9,944	4,003	3,220
Grand total	39,242	15,665	13,141

[a] The register of women was not given separately from that of the men. The number of women on enrollment has been substituted, as there is usually no material difference between the two sets of figures.

[b] Neither the number of women on register nor on enrollment was available. An estimate has been made of the number of women on register in relation to the total register of the school on the basis of the proportion that the number of women in average attendance formed of the total average attendance.

Location and designation of school	Women whose fathers were born in: Russia	United States	Germany	Ireland	Austria-Hungary [a]	Great Britain	Italy	Scandinavia	Roumania	Other countries	Women who did not state country of birth of father	All women
Manhattan and the Bronx												
High and trade schools												
East Side high	468	13	19	6	255	5	11	1	48	2	19	847
Harlem high	236	149	148	80	133	48	8	18	12	29	22	883
Morris high, mixed	59	120	139	40	33	21	2	6	6	5	22	453
New York high and trade	22	101	80	86	40	20	7	5	4	12	27	404
Elementary schools												
4	65	2	2	..	84	..	..	..	5	..	3	161
10	30	124	132	45	23	25	4	3	6	25	26	443
13	54	1	3	..	45	..	3	..	35	1	1	143
14	11	36	20	54	8	11	17	6	1	12	3	179
17	10	90	68	112	6	8	15	2	..	12	10	333
19	12	18	24	11	17	1	22	..	3	4	1	113
23	4	7	4	2	1	..	113	..	..	2	2	135
29	..	13	6	9	1	2	2	..	..	11	..	44
38	..	29	8	46	1	4	43	..	..	3	2	136
42	644	3	1	2	34	..	3	..	24	5	1	717
45	1	82	19	88	4	15	11	5	..	16	6	247
59	15	24	50	40	46	7	28	12	1	21	6	250
67	..	75	6	4	..	..	3	..	..	18	5	111
71	107	4	3	..	82	..	2	..	10	3	1	212
72	190	42	31	42	44	7	17	2	7	10	13	405
89	7	71	10	1	8	1	..	..	1	13	2	114
92	61	5	..	3	31	..	5	..	2	..	2	109
93	5	51	56	34	26	5	4	17	..	29	1	228
96	18	92	162	45	150	9	13	3	3	10	13	518
157	4	122	39	50	5	20	1	7	..	17	17	282
177	172	..	..	..	2	..	1	..	..	..	4	179
Total	2,195	1,274	1,030	800	1,079	209	335	87	168	260	209	7,646
All Brooklyn and Long Island City	784	1,634	1,103	644	281	330	154	207	41	153	164	5,495
Grand total	2,979	2,908	2,133	1,444	1,360	539	489	294	209	413	373	13,141

[a] Includes Bohemia.

TABLE D.—INDUSTRIES OF WOMEN ATTENDING PUBLIC EVENING SCHOOLS EMPLOYED IN MANUFACTURING AND MECHANICAL PURSUITS, BY TYPE OF SCHOOL, FOR MANHATTAN AND THE BRONX, AND FOR BROOKLYN AND LONG ISLAND CITY

Industry	WOMEN EMPLOYED AS SPECIFIED ATTENDING					All women
	Evening schools located in		Elementary evening schools	Evening trade schools	Evening high schools	
	Manhattan and the Bronx	Brooklyn and Long Island City				
Artificial flowers and feathers (total)	240	52	212	..	80	292
Men's clothing						
Men's tailored garments	46	23	68	..	1	69
Boys' tailored garments	5	3	7	..	1	8
Vests	12	6	17	..	1	18
Shirts	26	41	64	..	3	67
Neckwear	11	7	12	..	6	18
Collars and cuffs	1	3	3	..	1	4
Other furnishing goods	13	14	21	..	6	27
Total	114	97	192	..	19	211
Women's clothing						
Tailored garments	154	49	196	..	7	203
Dressmaking (custom and factory)	572	112	563	14	107	684
Dressmaking (private)	2	13	13	..	2	15
Shirtwaists	342	77	383	..	36	419
Children's clothing	50	23	63	..	10	73
Infants' clothing	13	10	17	..	6	23
Children's headwear	8	6	9	2	3	14
Muslin underwear	235	53	255	..	33	288
Petticoats (other than muslin)	21	4	21	..	4	25
Neckwear	86	23	80	1	28	109
Corsets	31	2	26	1	6	33
Other furnishing goods	20	22	36	1	5	42
Total	1,534	394	1,662	19	247	1,928
Confectionery, groceries, bakery products, and tobacco						
Confectionery	45	30	68	1	6	75
Chewing gum and licorice	..	10	9	1	..	10
Groceries	23	9	28	..	4	32
Bakery products	12	8	16	..	4	20
Tobacco, cigars, cigarettes	65	32	90	1	6	97
Total	145	89	211	3	20	234

TABLE D (Continued)

Fur, leather, rubber, hair goods, etc.						
Suit cases	4	1	5	..	..	5
Shoes	..	32	19	1	12	32
Gloves	7	34	27	..	14	41
Belts	9	6	15	..	..	15
Purses	10	5	14	..	1	15
Other leather goods	4	6	7	..	3	10
Rubber goods	8	9	11	..	6	17
Hair goods	63	17	72	..	8	80
Fur goods	15	1	15	..	1	16
Buttons	21	9	22	2	6	30
Canvas and sporting goods	1	5	4	..	2	6
Novelty goods	29	13	27	1	14	42
Other articles of bone, pearl, horn, etc.	27	8	27	..	8	35
Total	198	146	265	4	75	344
Millinery (total)	194	69	186	4	73	263
Miscellaneous needlework						
Hand and machine embroidery	113	27	122	..	18	140
Handkerchiefs	11	9	18	..	2	20
Curtains	7	6	12	..	1	13
Flags	1	3	1	..	3	4
Quilting	6	..	6	..	..	6
Umbrellas	6	..	6	..	..	6
Other miscellaneous needlework	20	23	33	1	9	43
Total	164	68	198	1	33	232
Printing and paper goods						
Printing and engraving	10	9	13	..	6	19
Stationery	9	18	19	..	8	27
Lithographing	10	11	17	..	4	21
Bookbinding	54	90	112	4	28	144
Photography	8	2	5	..	5	10
Paper boxes	82	51	124	..	9	133
Paper novelty goods	5	4	7	1	1	9
Patterns	5	4	5	1	3	9
Paper bags	3	1	3	..	1	4
Post cards	11	1	9	..	3	12
Sample cards	14	3	13	..	4	17
Other paper goods	4	8	10	1	1	12
Total	215	202	337	7	73	417

TABLE D (Continued)

Industry	Women employed as specified attending: Evening schools located in: Manhattan and the Bronx	Evening schools located in: Brooklyn and Long Island City	Elementary evening schools	Evening trade schools	Evening high schools	All women
Textiles						
Cotton fabrics	5	5	5	..	5	10
Silk goods	56	25	67	4	10	81
Woolen goods	4	2	3	..	3	6
Knit goods	16	67	68	1	14	83
Scarfs, shawls	5	4	8	..	1	9
Laces, veils	11	3	10	..	4	14
Braids, passementerie	18	26	36	1	7	44
Upholstery	7	1	8	..	..	8
Window shades	4	3	7	..	..	7
Flax, hemp, and jute goods	6	19	24	..	1	25
Carpets	1	3	3	1	..	4
Dyed and printed fabrics	2	..	1	..	1	2
Total	135	158	240	7	46	293
All other industries						
Stone, glass, and clay products	6	9	15	..	..	15
Metal goods	43	34	70	..	7	77
Electric supplies	8	1	5	..	4	9
Lanterns and lamp shades	3	6	6	3	..	9
Gold and silver goods and jewelry	8	10	15	1	2	18
Wood and cork goods	8	7	13	..	2	15
Soap, perfumery, etc.	6	12	14	1	3	18
Paints, dyes, and lead pencils	9	18	23	..	4	27
Drugs, chemicals, and ink	15	25	26	6	8	40
Dental supplies	6	..	6	..	..	6
Laundry work, cleaning, and dyeing	42	18	56	..	4	60
Hats (not otherwise specified)	2	9	9	..	2	11
Total	156	149	258	11	36	305
Grand total	3,095	1,424	3,761	56	702	4,519

TABLE E.—LENGTH OF NOON RECESS FOR WOMEN ATTENDING PUBLIC EVENING SCHOOLS EMPLOYED IN MANUFACTURING AND MECHANICAL PURSUITS AND IN TRADE AND TRANSPORTATION

Length of noon recess	WOMEN EMPLOYED IN			
	Manufacturing and mechanical pursuits		Trade and transportation	
	Number	Per cent	Number	Per cent
Less than 30 minutes	19	.5	12	.3
30 minutes and less than 45 minutes	1,541	43.5	405	9.9
45 minutes and less than 60 minutes	609	17.2	972	23.8
60 minutes or more	1,378	38.8	2,693	66.0
Total	3,547[a]	100.0	4,082[a]	100.0

[a] Data relative to hours of work have been tabulated only for women who were employed at date of investigation. Of the 4,519 engaged in manufacturing and mechanical pursuits, 190 were unemployed, three worked at home, 658 were in an evening school for which the data as to hours were found to be inaccurate and were not tabulated, and of the 3,668 remaining, 121 did not supply information. Of the 4,505 in trade and transportation, 317 were unemployed, one worked at home, 22 were in an evening school for which the data were not tabulated, and of the 4,165 remaining, 83 did not supply information. One in trade and transportation worked only half days and had no noon recess.

TABLE F.—NORMAL DAILY HOURS OF WORK OF WOMEN ATTENDING PUBLIC EVENING SCHOOLS AND EMPLOYED IN MANUFACTURING AND MECHANICAL PURSUITS, BY MAIN GROUPS OF OCCUPATIONS

Daily hours of work	WOMEN WORKING SPECIFIED HOURS IN										
	Artificial flower and feather making	Making of men's clothing	Making of women's clothing	Work on confectionery, groceries, bakery products, tobacco, etc.	Work on fur, leather, rubber, hair goods, etc.	Millinery	Miscellaneous needlework	Work on printing and paper goods	Work on textiles	Other manufacturing and mechanical pursuits	All manufacturing and mechanical pursuits
Number working											
Less than 8 hours	37	4	18	8	6	15	3	17	9	12	129
8 hours	54	14	63	28	36	22	29	65	48	42	401
More than 8 hours and less than 9 hours	73	20	151	33	39	77	35	82	26	43	579
9 hours and less than 10 hours	79	66	982	78	153	82	115	176	87	132	1,950
10 hours or more	3	47	91	58	45	5	12	16	89	45	411
Total	246	151	1,305	205	279	201	194	356	259	274	3,470[a]
Per cent working											
Less than 8 hours	15	3	1	4	2	8	2	5	3	4	4
8 hours	22	9	5	14	13	11	15	18	19	15	12
More than 8 hours and less than 9 hours	30	13	12	16	14	38	18	23	10	16	16
9 hours and less than 10 hours	32	44	75	38	55	40	59	50	34	49	56
10 hours or more	1	31	7	28	16	3	6	4	34	16	12
Total	100	100	100	100	100	100	100	100	100	100	100

[a] Of 4,519, the total, 193 were unemployed or were working at home, 658 were in an evening school for which the data as to hours were found to be inaccurate and were not tabulated, and 198 did not supply information.

TABLE G.—AGES OF WOMEN ATTENDING PUBLIC EVENING SCHOOLS, BY PRINCIPAL OCCUPATIONAL GROUPS AND BY SELECTED OCCUPATIONS

Occupation	NUMBER OF WOMEN					PER CENT OF WOMEN				
	Less than 16 years	16 years and less than 18 years	18 years and less than 21 years	21 years or more	Total	Less than 16 years	16 years and less than 18 years	18 years and less than 21 years	21 years or more	Total
Principal occupational group										
Manufacturing and mechanical pursuits	1,044	1,606	1,225	574	4,449	23.5	36.1	27.5	12.9	100.0
Trade and transportation	740	1,647	1,247	842	4,476	16.5	36.8	27.9	18.8	100.0
Domestic and personal service	41	65	88	310	504	8.1	12.9	17.5	61.5	100.0
Professional service	4	17	35	132	188	2.1	9.0	18.6	70.3	100.0
No gainful occupation[a]	803	849	533	1,185	3,370	23.8	25.2	15.8	35.2	100.0
Total	2,632	4,184	3,128	3,043	12,987[b]	20.3	32.2	24.1	23.4	100.0
Selected occupation										
Artificial flower making	103	128	43	14	288	35.8	44.4	14.9	4.9	100.0
Making of men's clothing	41	85	60	22	208	19.7	40.9	28.8	10.6	100.0
Dressmaking	102	199	220	145	666	15.3	29.9	33.0	21.8	100.0
Shirtwaist making	44	156	186	25	411	10.7	38.0	45.2	6.1	100.0
Work on white goods	54	102	100	30	286	18.9	35.6	35.0	10.5	100.0
Work on confectionery, food, tobacco, etc.	72	75	55	30	232	31.0	32.4	23.7	12.9	100.0
Work on hair goods	25	31	19	4	79	31.6	39.2	24.1	5.1	100.0
Button making	11	15	5	2	33	33.3	45.4	15.2	6.1	100.0
Millinery	59	102	62	36	259	22.8	39.4	23.9	13.9	100.0
Miscellaneous needlework	64	85	50	30	229	28.0	37.1	21.8	13.1	100.0
Bookbinding	41	50	31	21	143	28.7	34.9	21.7	14.7	100.0
Paper box making	42	53	29	4	128	32.8	41.4	22.7	3.1	100.0
Work on textiles	96	99	54	41	290	33.1	34.2	18.6	14.1	100.0
Stenography, bookkeeping	110	633	630	433	1,806	6.1	35.0	34.9	24.0	100.0
Clerical and office work	318	650	466	308	1,742	18.2	37.3	26.8	17.7	100.0
Work in stores	264	257	111	68	700	37.7	36.7	15.9	9.7	100.0
Teaching	...	...	22	110	132	....	....	16.7	83.3	100.0

[a] For further explanation, see footnote, p. 36.

[b] Of the 13,141 women included in the study, 154 did not supply information.

TABLE H.—AGE AT LEAVING DAY SCHOOL OF WOMEN ATTENDING PUBLIC EVENING SCHOOLS, EMPLOYED IN MANUFACTURING AND MECHANICAL PURSUITS, BY MAIN GROUPS OF OCCUPATIONS

Occupation	WOMEN WHO LEFT SCHOOL WHEN						Women who never attended day school	Women who stated age	Women who did not state age	All women
	Less than 14 years	14 years and less than 15 years	15 years and less than 16 years	16 years and less than 17 years	17 years and less than 18 years	18 years or more				
Number										
Artificial flower and feather making	21	101	65	25	3	2	2	219	73	292
Making of men's clothing	25	75	15	8	2	1	2	128	83	211
Making of women's clothing	233	458	216	71	18	16	14	1,026	902	1,928
Work on confectionery, food, tobacco, etc.	43	90	50	11	1	1	2	198	36	234
Work on furs, leather, rubber, hair goods, etc.	24	136	66	27	4	4	2	263	81	344
Millinery	32	72	51	28	8	4	2	197	66	263
Miscellaneous needlework	26	96	45	12	3	2	..	184	48	232
Work on printing and paper goods	31	209	82	25	3	2	2	354	63	417
Work on textiles	38	131	54	19	4	..	4	250	43	293
Other occupations in manufacturing and mechanical pursuits	43	131	63	19	6	3	4	269	36	305
Total	516	1,499	707	245	52	35	34	3,088	1,431[a]	4,519
Per cent										
Artificial flower and feather making	9.6	46.1	29.7	11.4	1.4	.9	.9	100.0		
Making of men's clothing	19.5	58.5	11.7	6.3	1.6	.8	1.6	100.0		
Making of women's clothing	22.7	44.6	21.0	6.9	1.8	1.6	1.4	100.0		
Work on confectionery, food, tobacco, etc.	21.7	45.4	25.3	5.6	.5	.5	1.0	100.0		
Work on furs, leather, rubber, hair goods, etc.	9.1	51.7	25.1	10.3	1.5	1.5	.8	100.0		
Millinery	16.2	36.6	25.9	14.2	4.1	2.0	1.0	100.0		
Miscellaneous needlework	14.1	52.2	24.5	6.5	1.6	1.1	...	100.0		
Work on printing and paper goods	8.7	59.0	23.2	7.1	.8	.6	.6	100.0		
Work on textiles	15.2	52.4	21.6	7.6	1.6	...	1.6	100.0		
Other occupations in manufacturing and mechanical pursuits	16.0	48.7	23.4	7.1	2.2	1.1	1.5	100.0		
Total	16.7	48.6	22.9	7.9	1.7	1.1	1.1	100.0		

[a] Including 827 in evening schools for which data on age at leaving day school were incomplete and were not tabulated.

TABLE I.—YEARS OF ATTENDANCE AT HIGH SCHOOL FOR WOMEN ATTENDING PUBLIC EVENING SCHOOLS, WHO LAST ATTENDED DAY SCHOOL IN NEW YORK PUBLIC HIGH SCHOOLS, BY PRINCIPAL OCCUPATIONAL GROUPS

Years of attendance	WOMEN EMPLOYED IN					All women
	Manufacturing and mechanical pursuits	Trade and transportation	Domestic and personal service	Professional service	No gainful occupation[a]	
Number who attended						
Less than 1 year	59	274	2	2	188	525
1 year and less than 2 years	41	367	1	5	173	587
2 years and less than 3 years	23	193	1	4	109	330
3 years and less than 4 years	5	84	..	9	36	134
4 years and less than 5 years	2	27	1	91	33	154
5 years or more	2	2	..	4	3	11
Total	132	947	5	115	542	1,741[b]
Per cent who attended						
Less than 1 year	44	29	40	2	34	30
1 year and less than 2 years	31	39	20	4	32	33
2 years and less than 3 years	17	20	20	3	20	19
3 years and less than 4 years	4	9	..	8	7	8
4 years and less than 5 years	2	3	20	80	6	9
5 years or more	2	..[c]	..	3	1	1
Total	100	100	100	100	100	100

[a] For further explanation, see footnote, p. 36.

[b] Of the 1,803 who last attended day school in a New York City public high school, 62 did not state number of years of attendance.

[c] Less than .5 per cent.

TABLE J.—AGES, NATIVITY, SCHOOLING, AND HOURS OF EMPLOYMENT BY SELECTED OCCUPATIONS IN TRADE AND TRANSPORTATION AND IN MANUFACTURING AND MECHANICAL PURSUITS, OF WOMEN ATTENDING PUBLIC EVENING SCHOOLS

	WOMEN EMPLOYED IN TRADE AND TRANSPORTATION			WOMEN EMPLOYED IN MANUFACTURING AND MECHANICAL PURSUITS						
	Clerical and office work	Stenography and book-keeping	Work in stores	Artificial flower and feather making	Book-binding	Dress-making	Millinery	Paper box making	Shirt-waist making	Work on white goods
Age of women										
Less than 16 years	318	110	264	103	41	102	59	42	44	54
16 years and less than 18 years	650	633	257	128	50	199	102	53	156	102
18 years and less than 21 years	466	630	111	43	31	220	62	29	186	100
21 years or more	308	433	68	14	21	145	36	4	25	30
Total women reporting	1,742	1,806	700	288	143	666	259	128	411	286
Women not reporting	12	7	9	4	1	16	4	2	8	2
Total	1,754	1,813	709	292	144	682	263	130	419	288
Nativity of fathers of women										
Russia	225	402	94	134	8	259	91	48	319	177
United States	485	375	181	17	57	65	47	27	6	9
Germany	297	313	118	15	29	72	31	15	9	8
Ireland	283	188	169	5	31	57	16	10	1	10
Austria-Hungary[a]	160	241	45	70	2	88	38	7	50	52
Great Britain	109	92	31	2	5	17	3	6	1	..
Italy	24	14	17	23	7	51	7	15	7	14
Scandinavia	44	41	16	2	..	7	7	..	..	..
Roumania	19	33	6	10	..	14	12	1	15	11
Other countries	50	43	16	7	1	33	5	1	2	1
Total women reporting	1,696	1,742	693	285	140	663	257	130	410	282
Women not reporting	58	71	16	7	4	19	6	..	9	6
Total	1,754	1,813	709	292	144	682	263	130	419	288

[a] Includes Bohemia.

TABLE 5 (Continued)

	WOMEN EMPLOYED IN TRADE AND TRANSPORTATION			WOMEN EMPLOYED IN MANUFACTURING AND MECHANICAL PURSUITS						
	Clerical and office work	Stenography and book-keeping	Work in stores	Artificial flower and feather making	Book-binding	Dress-making	Millinery	Paper box making	Shirt-waist making	Work on white goods
Nativity of women										
United States	1,527	1,485	576	123	133	243	136	75	41	64
Russia	72	124	57	101	2	232	73	41	307	162
Austria-Hungary[a]	37	61	19	40	..	68	20	5	44	36
Germany	18	27	11	4	..	17	6	2	4	1
Italy	7	5	10	9	3	36	3	2	4	4
Ireland	18	18	16	..	3	14	..	1	..	1
Great Britain	24	27	11	3	2	5	3	3	..	2
Roumania	6	18	2	8	..	27	14	..	15	15
Scandinavia	11	11	3	..	..	3	1	..	..	..
Other countries	24	24	..	1	..	28	5	1	1	1
Total women reporting	1,744	1,800	705	289	143	673	261	130	416	286
Women not reporting	10	13	4	3	1	9	2	..	3	2
Total	1,754	1,813	709	292	144	682	263	130	419	288
Last school attended										
New York City public school	1,375	1,512	483	218	85	229	154	69	96	116
New York City parochial or private school	236	119	143	10	47	50	19	25	7	10
School in the United States outside New York City	67	104	18	5	1	22	9	2	4	3
School in a foreign country	39	49	34	32	4	229	51	12	155	75
No day school	2	..	4	3	..	33	3	5	53	28
Total women reporting	1,719	1,784	682	268	137	563	236	113	315	232
Women not reporting	35	29	27	24	7	119	27	17	104	56
Total	1,754	1,813	709	292	144	682	263	130	419	288

[a] Includes Bohemia.

Age at leaving school										
Less than 14 years . .	135	186	66	21	14	96	32	7	43	23
14 years and less than 15 years	608	530	327	101	68	181	72	65	51	76
15 years and less than 16 years	503	484	172	65	33	86	51	17	35	31
16 years and less than 17 years	228	269	63	25	10	33	28	3	8	8
17 years and less than 18 years	75	92	14	3	2	9	8	1	2	2
18 years or more . . .	30	49	4	2	1	12	4	..	1	..
Never attended school .	2	..	3	2	..	6	2	2	3	2
Total women reporting	1,581	1,610	649	219	128	423	197	95	143	142
Women not reporting	173	203	60	73	16	259	66	35	276	146
Total	1,754	1,813	709	292	144	682	263	130	419	288
Total daily hours of work										
Less than 8 hours . .	488	924	17	37	6	5	15	1	2	2
8 hours	301	313	11	54	32	14	22	12	8	10
More than 8 hours and less than 8½ hours . . .	122	69	13	18	6	11	4	5	2	1
8½ hours and less than 9 hours	334	211	310	55	30	52	73	8	12	11
9 hours and less than 9½ hours	253	92	226	71	32	322	72	28	161	53
9½ hours and less than 10 hours	63	12	25	8	22	71	10	36	42	82
10 hours or more . . .	19	16	22	3	2	19	5	10	7	28
Total women reporting	1,580	1,637	624	246	130	494	201	100	234	187
Women not reporting	174	176	85	46	14	188	62	30	185	101
Total	1,754	1,813	709	292	144	682	263	130	419	288

TABLE J (Continued)

	WOMEN EMPLOYED IN TRADE AND TRANSPORTATION			WOMEN EMPLOYED IN MANUFACTURING AND MECHANICAL PURSUITS						
	Clerical and office work	Stenography and book-keeping	Work in stores	Artificial flower and feather making	Book-binding	Dress-making	Millinery	Paper box making	Shirt-waist making	Work on white goods
Age of women Per cent										
Less than 16 years	18.3	6.1	37.7	35.8	28.7	15.3	22.8	32.8	10.7	18.8
16 years and less than 18 years	37.3	35.0	36.7	44.4	34.9	29.9	39.4	41.4	37.9	35.6
18 years and less than 21 years	26.7	34.9	15.9	14.9	21.7	33.0	23.9	22.7	45.3	35.0
21 years or more	17.7	24.0	9.7	4.9	14.7	21.8	13.9	3.1	6.1	10.5
Total reporting	100.0	100.0	100.0	100.0	100.0	100.0	100.0	100.0	100.0	100.0
Nativity of fathers of women Per cent										
Russia	13.3	23.1	13.6	46.9	5.7	39.1	35.4	36.9	77.8	62.8
United States	28.6	21.5	26.1	6.0	40.7	9.8	18.3	20.8	1.5	3.2
Germany	17.5	18.0	17.0	5.3	20.7	10.8	12.1	11.5	2.2	2.8
Ireland	16.7	10.8	24.3	1.8	22.2	8.6	6.2	7.7	.2	3.5
Austria-Hungary [a]	9.4	13.8	6.5	24.5	1.4	13.3	14.8	5.4	12.2	18.4
Great Britain	6.4	5.3	4.5	.7	3.6	2.6	1.2	4.6	.2	...
Italy	1.4	.8	2.5	8.1	5.0	7.7	2.7	11.5	1.7	5.0
Scandinavia	2.6	2.3	2.3	.7	...	1.0	2.7	...	...	...
Roumania	1.1	1.9	.9	3.5	...	2.1	4.7	.8	3.7	3.9
Other countries	3.0	2.5	2.3	2.5	.7	5.0	1.9	.8	.5	.4
Total reporting	100.0	100.0	100.0	100.0	100.0	100.0	100.0	100.0	100.0	100.0

[a] Includes Bohemia.

Nativity of women Per cent										
United States	87.6	82.5	81.7	42.6	93.0	36.1	52.1	57.7	9.9	22.4
Russia	4.2	6.9	8.0	35.0	1.4	34.5	28.0	31.5	73.7	56.8
Austria-Hungary [a]	2.1	3.4	2.7	13.8	...	10.1	7.7	3.9	10.6	12.6
Germany	1.0	1.5	1.6	1.4	...	2.5	2.3	1.5	1.0	.3
Italy	1.4	.3	1.4	3.1	2.1	5.4	1.1	1.5	1.0	1.4
Ireland	1.0	1.0	2.3	...	2.1	2.1	...	.8	...	.3
Great Britain	1.4	1.5	1.6	1.0	1.4	.7	1.1	2.3	...	.7
Roumania	.3	1.0	.3	2.8	...	4.0	5.4	...	3.6	5.2
Scandinavia	.6	.6	.4	...	...	.4	.4	...	...	...
Other countries	1.4	1.3	...	.3	...	4.2	1.9	.8	.2	.3
Total reporting	100.0	100.0	100.0	100.0	100.0	100.0	100.0	100.0	100.0	100.0
Last school attended Per cent										
New York City public school	80.0	84.8	70.8	81.3	62.1	40.7	65.5	61.1	30.5	50.0
New York City parochial or private school	13.7	6.7	21.0	3.7	34.3	8.8	8.1	22.1	2.2	4.3
School in the United States outside New York City	3.9	5.8	2.6	1.9	.7	3.9	3.8	1.8	1.3	1.3
School in a foreign country	2.3	2.7	5.0	12.0	2.9	40.7	21.7	10.6	49.2	32.3
No day school	.1	...	.6	1.1	...	5.9	.9	4.4	16.8	12.1
Total reporting	100.0	100.0	100.0	100.0	100.0	100.0	100.0	100.0	100.0	100.0
Age at leaving school Per cent										
Less than 14 years	8.5	11.6	10.2	9.6	10.9	22.7	16.2	7.4	30.1	16.2
14 years	38.5	32.9	50.3	46.1	53.1	42.9	36.5	68.4	35.6	53.6
15 years and less than 16 years	31.9	30.1	26.5	29.7	25.8	20.3	26.0	17.8	24.5	21.8
16 years and less than 17 years	14.4	16.7	9.7	11.4	7.8	7.8	14.2	3.2	5.6	5.6
17 years and less than 18 years	4.7	5.7	2.2	1.4	1.6	2.1	4.1	1.1	1.4	1.4
18 years or more	1.9	3.0	.6	.9	.8	2.8	2.0	...	.7	...
Never attended day school	.1	...	.5	.9	...	1.4	1.0	2.1	2.1	1.4
Total reporting	100.0	100.0	100.0	100.0	100.0	100.0	100.0	100.0	100.0	100.0

[a] Includes Bohemia.

TABLE J—(Continued)

	WOMEN EMPLOYED IN TRADE AND TRANSPORTATION			WOMEN EMPLOYED IN MANUFACTURING AND MECHANICAL PURSUITS						
	Clerical and office work	Stenography and bookkeeping	Work in stores	Artificial flower and feather making	Bookbinding	Dressmaking	Millinery	Paper box making	Shirtwaist making	Work on white goods
Total daily hours of work										
Per cent										
Less than 8 hours	30.9	56.5	2.7	15.0	4.6	1.0	7.5	1.0	.9	1.1
8 hours	19.1	19.1	1.8	21.9	24.6	2.8	10.9	12.0	3.4	5.3
More than 8 hours and less than 8½ hours	7.7	4.2	2.1	7.3	4.6	2.2	2.0	5.0	.9	.5
8½ hours and less than 9 hours	21.1	12.9	49.7	22.4	23.1	10.6	36.3	8.0	5.1	5.9
9 hours and less than 9½ hours	16.0	5.6	36.2	28.9	24.6	65.2	35.8	28.0	68.8	28.3
9½ hours and less than 10 hours	4.0	.7	4.0	3.3	17.0	14.4	5.0	36.0	17.9	43.9
10 hours or more	1.2	1.0	3.5	1.2	1.5	3.8	2.5	10.0	3.0	15.0
Total reporting	100.0	100.0	100.0	100.0	100.0	100.0	100.0	100.0	100.0	100.0

TABLE K.*—GRADE AT LEAVING SCHOOL, BY MAIN GROUPS OF OCCUPATIONS IN MANUFACTURING AND MECHANICAL PURSUITS AND BY SELECTED OCCUPATIONS FOR WOMEN ATTENDING PUBLIC EVENING SCHOOLS, WHO LAST ATTENDED DAY SCHOOL IN A NEW YORK PUBLIC SCHOOL

Occupation	WOMEN WHO LEFT SCHOOL IN					Women who stated grade[a]	Women who did not state grade[a]	All women
	Grades below the fifth	Fifth grade	Sixth grade	Seventh grade	Eighth grade or above			
Main group of occupations in manufacturing and mechanical pursuits								
Artificial flower and feather making	4	18	31	43	99	195	23	218
Making of men's clothing	5	16	20	16	20	77	7	84
Making of women's clothing	26	60	117	153	237	593	74	667
Work on confectionery, food, tobacco, etc.	8	12	27	32	43	122	9	131
Work on furs, leather, rubber, hair goods, etc.	5	17	36	58	72	188	22	210
Millinery	3	6	19	32	85	145	9	154
Miscellaneous needlework	4	10	21	31	54	120	6	126
Work on printing and paper goods	7	24	54	65	95	245	8	253
Work on textiles	5	16	36	53	56	166	20	186
Other occupations	7	17	36	45	71	176	7	183
Total	74	196	397	528	832	2,027	185	2,212
Selected occupation								
Dressmaking	8	22	30	62	97	219	10	229
Shirtwaist making	3	10	21	18	25	77	19	96
Work on white goods	5	9	19	24	36	93	23	116
Work on hair goods	2	7	10	13	5	37	6	43
Button making	2	..	6	4	9	21	1	22
Bookbinding	3	2	14	21	42	82	3	85
Paper box making	2	12	22	16	13	65	4	69
Stenography, bookkeeping	1	4	22	61	1,418	1,506	6	1,512
Clerical and office work	4	15	60	136	1,143	1,358	11	1,369
Work in stores	6	17	81	110	250	464	10	474
Teaching	..	..	..	1	111	112	...	112

* Table continued on following page. See footnote, page 208.

TABLE K (Continued)

Occupation	Women who left school in: Grades below the fifth	Fifth grade	Sixth grade	Seventh grade	Eighth grade or above	Women who stated grade [a]	Women who did not state grade [a]	All women
Main group of occupations in manufacturing and mechanical pursuits								
Per cent								
Artificial flower and feather making	2.1	9.2	15.9	22.0	50.8	100.0		
Making of men's clothing	6.4	20.8	26.0	20.8	26.0	100.0		
Making of women's clothing	4.4	10.1	19.7	25.8	40.0	100.0		
Work on confectionery, food, tobacco, etc.	6.6	9.8	22.1	26.2	35.3	100.0		
Work on furs, leather, rubber, hair goods, etc.	2.7	9.0	19.1	30.9	38.3	100.0		
Millinery	2.1	4.1	13.1	22.1	58.6	100.0		
Miscellaneous needlework	3.3	8.3	17.5	25.9	45.0	100.0		
Work on printing and paper goods	2.9	9.8	22.0	26.5	38.8	100.0		
Work on textiles	3.0	9.6	21.7	31.9	33.8	100.0		
Other occupations	4.0	9.7	20.4	25.6	40.3	100.0		
Total	3.6	9.7	19.6	26.0	41.1	100.0		
Selected occupation								
Per cent								
Dressmaking	3.7	10.0	13.7	28.3	44.3	100.0		
Shirtwaist making	3.9	13.0	27.2	23.4	32.5	100.0		
Work on white goods	5.4	9.7	20.4	25.8	38.7	100.0		
Work on hair goods	5.4	18.9	27.0	35.2	13.5	100.0		
Button making	9.5	....	28.6	19.1	42.8	100.0		
Bookbinding	3.7	2.4	17.1	25.6	51.2	100.0		
Paper box making	3.1	18.5	33.8	24.6	20.0	100.0		
Stenography, bookkeeping	.1	.3	1.5	4.1	94.0	100.0		
Clerical and office work	.3	1.1	4.4	10.0	84.2	100.0		
Work in stores	1.3	3.7	17.4	23.7	53.9	100.0		
Teaching	....	....	....	.9	99.1	100.0		

[a] Including those in the two schools for which information on this point was omitted. (See footnote [b] to Table 17, p. 94.)

TABLE L.—MONTHS IN WHICH 1,127 WOMEN ATTENDING PUBLIC EVENING HIGH SCHOOLS DROPPED OUT, BY PRINCIPAL OCCUPATIONAL GROUPS AND BY AGES

Occupational group and age	Women dropping out in								Women remaining in May	All women
	September	October	November	December	January	February	March	April		
Occupational group										
Manufacturing and mechanical pursuits	3	22	13	8	11	4	7	4	50	122
Trade and transportation	30	132	101	52	55	53	42	27	337	829
Domestic and personal service	..	2	..	..	..	1	..	..	7	10
Professional service	1	3	2	1	1	1	1	1	8	19
No gainful occupation [a]	12	13	9	6	16	9	4	3	75	147
Total	46	172	125	67	83	68	54	35	477	1,127 [b]
Age										
Less than 16 years	11	24	12	6	16	11	5	5	67	157
16 years and less than 18 years	13	60	45	20	31	22	21	8	183	403
18 years and less than 21 years	14	57	42	26	23	22	15	11	134	344
21 years or more	8	31	25	15	13	13	13	11	93	222
Not reported	..	..	1	..	..	..	..	..	..	1
Total	46	172	125	67	83	68	54	35	477	1,127

[a] For further explanation, see footnote, p. 36.

[b] Attendance figures were secured for 1,233 of the 4,862 women included in this study and attending public evening high schools. Of these 1,233 pupils, 106 did not enter until the second or third month of the term.

TABLE M.—MONTHS IN WHICH 973 WOMEN ATTENDING FOUR PUBLIC EVENING ELEMENTARY SCHOOLS DROPPED OUT, BY PRINCIPAL OCCUPATIONAL GROUPS AND BY AGES, MANHATTAN BOROUGH

Occupational group and age	Women dropping out in					Women remaining in March	All women
	October	November	December	January	February		
Occupational group							
Manufacturing and mechanical pursuits	39	50	15	44	13	323	484
Trade and transportation	36	28	22	21	8	148	263
Domestic and personal service	2	3	2	1	1	12	21
Professional service	1	..	..	..	..	3	4
No gainful occupation[a]	10	21	22	11	10	127	201
Total	88	102	61	77	32	613	973[b]
Age							
Less than 16 years	33	34	10	16	8	158	259
16 years and less that 18 years	30	34	28	30	14	207	343
18 years and less than 21 years	17	22	9	19	4	145	216
21 years or more	8	11	13	11	6	90	139
Not reported	..	1	1	1	..	13	16
Total	88	102	61	77	32	613	973

[a] For further explanation, see footnote, p. 36.

[b] Attendance figures were secured for 973 of the 1,044 women included in this study and attending public evening elementary schools numbers 14, 23, 71, 96 in Manhattan, in which data could be secured for the full term of six months.

TABLE N.—MONTHS IN WHICH 1,993 WOMEN ATTENDING 13 PUBLIC EVENING ELEMENTARY SCHOOLS DROPPED OUT, BY PRINCIPAL OCCUPATIONAL GROUPS AND BY AGES, MANHATTAN BOROUGH

Occupational group and age	WOMEN DROPPING OUT IN				Women remaining in February [a]	All women
	October	November	December	January		
Occupational group						
Manufacturing and mechanical pursuits	46	100	97	83	564	890
Trade and transportation	31	64	50	34	304	483
Domestic and personal service	14	38	23	17	123	215
Professional service	..	1	..	2	2	5
No gainful occupation [b]	21	51	51	40	237	400
Total	112	254	221	176	1,230	1,993 [c]
Age						
Less than 16 years	38	53	46	36	328	501
16 years and less than 18 years	23	83	65	47	379	597
18 years and less than 21 years	25	52	41	40	255	413
21 years or more	26	66	58	41	266	457
Not reported	..	..	11	12	2	25
Total	112	254	221	176	1,230	1,993

[a] Attendance figures were secured only through February, not through March.

[b] For further explanation, see footnote, p. 36.

[c] Attendance figures were secured for 1,993 of the 2,394 women included in this study and attending public evening elementary schools numbers 4, 13, 17, 19, 29, 38, 45, 59, 67, 72, 89, 92, 93 in Manhattan, in which attendance figures were secured through the month of February only.

APPENDIX II

MEMORANDUM REGARDING A SYSTEM OF EVENING SCHOOL RECORDS

THE following suggestions are offered by the Committee on Women's Work of the Russell Sage Foundation at the invitation of Dr. John H. Haaren, associate city superintendent in charge of evening schools in New York. As the Committee on Women's Work is concerned with investigations of women in industry, not with school administration, a prefatory word of explanation as to the reasons for presenting this memorandum is desirable.*

The suggestions are based on the experience of agents of the committee in handling the present school record books and cards in the course of an investigation of working girls enrolled in public evening schools in Manhattan, Bronx, and Brooklyn during the winter of 1910–11. It was a study, not of the schools, but of the pupils,—age, nationality, previous schooling, present occupation, and hours of work. The method, made possible by the co-operation of Dr. Haaren and the principals, was to have cards filled out by English-speaking girls attending the classes on a given night in the autumn when attendance is at a maximum. (See card No. 1, reproduced p. 186.) The total number secured was 13,737. In the spring, investigators returned to the schools in Manhattan and the Bronx to secure information about the attendance of a large

* This memorandum was submitted to Dr. John H. Haaren, associate city superintendent in charge of evening schools, and later to Dr. Albert Shiels, district superintendent in charge of evening schools. The main suggestions were adopted and a 5 by 8 card record system was introduced into the evening elementary schools in 1912. These are now in use throughout the city.

proportion of the girls who had filled these cards. This information was obtained directly from the teachers' roll books, and the work of copying it made unavoidable a close examination of the present system of record keeping.

The aim of the investigation was twofold. The analysis of the occupations and hours of work of a large group of working women affords an excellent foundation for a more intensive study of women in industry. At the same time the study of the women who are now seeking more education in the public schools throws light on the types which would probably be represented in the continuation schools advocated as an important part of a system of industrial education. Furthermore, many vexed problems of evening school administration are traceable to the hours of labor and other work conditions affecting day after day the welfare of evening school pupils. Thus, although the investigation was undertaken primarily as part of a study of women in industry, the results have convinced us that more information regarding the individual girl or boy, woman or man enrolled in evening classes would have some important results for the schools. We believe that a uniform record system would aid the teachers in studying their pupils and in meeting their individual needs, that it would result in greater economy of time in preparing the required statistical reports, that it would afford data for a solution of some vexed problems of evening school administration, and that it would bring to the schools a body of information of incalculable value in working out a program of industrial education.

In other words, the sort of card record system now recognized as important in day school work may well be tried out in evening schools. In the evening schools the record would include not only facts about the personal history and schooling of the pupil, but also facts about the daily industrial environment. It is to provide for such study of individuals that we would suggest the consideration of some possible changes in the present method of record keeping.

PRESENT METHODS OF KEEPING RECORDS*

I. Elementary Evening Schools

No uniform book or other form is provided. The information secured is determined mainly by the weekly and yearly statistical reports which the department of education requires. When a pupil applies for admission the principal or clerk records the date of application, name, address, occupation, age, and last school attended. Blank books of various kinds are used, possibly one designed for day schools, or any other which the principal may have at hand.

The method in some schools is slightly different. In addition to the admission book one principal keeps the detailed record of attendance of each pupil and the date of discharge. Another has lists filled by each teacher giving the facts about attendance for each of her pupils. Other principals keep in their offices only the total figures of attendance in each class.

The teachers' records in all the elementary evening schools in Manhattan, except two, are kept in roll books printed for day schools or in blank books ruled and cut by the teacher. These books contain the name, address, age, and sometimes, though rarely, the occupation of each pupil. The daily attendance is indicated by a slanting line in a ruled square. In the roll books printed for the day schools, spaces are provided for daily attendance for five months, the length of a term in day school. As the evening elementary schools are always open six months, from October to March inclusive, and sometimes into April, the marking of attendance in the sixth or seventh month becomes a problem to be solved by the ingenuity of each teacher. Some use again the spaces of the last two months, slanting the lines in the opposite direction. Others check an improvised set of squares on the opposite page. Others copy all the names again in another

* This refers to the school year of 1910–11.

part of the book, thus separating the record of attendance of each girl in a very inconvenient way.

In one school, the inconvenience of this method has led to the introduction of a card record system, provided by the principal at her own expense. Another principal in a nearby school adopted the following plan this winter: A 3 by 5 card is used, printed by means of a rubber stamp. On the front are the facts about the pupil, as follows: Date of admission, class, name, address, parent, nationality, last school, last grade, occupation, date of discharge, attendance first term, second term. On the back is space for the daily record of attendance, with a ruled square for each day of the month. When a pupil is discharged, her card is filed in the principal's office. Obviously, in view of the great fluctuation in attendance in the evening schools, the card record's adaptability to changes is a great advantage over the book in which a name can only be crossed out, and continues to cumber the pages for the rest of the year.

Thus the situation may be summed up by saying that no uniform system of records has yet been devised for the elementary evening schools. The result is inconvenience, loss of the teachers' time, danger of inaccuracy in making statistical reports, and the loss of much valuable information, some of which is now secured by principals and teachers but not made available because not recorded in a uniform and convenient way.

II. Evening High Schools

A uniform card record system is already installed in the evening high schools, and its use there gives promise of the development of a similar system in the elementary schools.

When a pupil applies for admission, a card, 3 by 5 inches in size, is filed in the principal's office. The teacher's record form for marking attendance is of the same size. The attendance is not marked by months but in groups of 10 evenings to aid the teacher in reporting the number of pupils attending 1–10 evenings, 10–20, 20–30, and so forth. The objection to it is that the number of possible evenings of attendance varies from month to month, and so it is difficult to keep track of the date which each square represents. For example, in the past winter, the number of possible evenings of attendance was 16 in October, 16 in November, 17 in January. A Hudson-Fulton celebration, or Lincoln's Birthday on Friday instead of Monday would change this count. The teachers say that this is confusing and necessitates a guide card with dates inserted in each square. Aside from this possible objection, and some possible suggestions regarding the information secured, the experience of the evening high schools seems to justify the card record system.

The Use of the Records. The records are the basis of the statistical reports to the department of education, and according to numbers reported the superintendents decide whether to continue or to disband a class. If the average attendance in a class falls below 15 the class is disbanded and the teacher loses her position. The weekly reports show the numbers attending each class each night in the week. The annual statistical report made by each principal shows the average attendance in each class each week of the school year, total number applying for admission to the school and never attending, number attending certain specified numbers of nights, 1–10, 10–20, 20–30, and so forth, total number on register in school year, number in each age group, 14–16, 16–18, 18–21, 21 and over, and the attendance of boys and girls aged fourteen to sixteen. These last figures concern the enforcement of the compulsory education law requiring all boys (not girls) between the ages of fourteen and sixteen to attend evening school if they have not graduated from elementary school.

Importance of Individual Records in Evening Schools. The importance of individual records in day schools is now widely discussed by school men, and uniform systems are being introduced. Very little attention, however, seems to have been given to possible plans for individual records in evening schools. On the contrary, according to the opinion of some principals, the fact that the test of a teacher's success is an average attendance of 15 or more has tended to obscure the importance of the individual. Yet there would seem to be very definite reasons for keeping track of each pupil in night school.

It is characteristic of night schools that their pupils are heterogeneous in such important conditions as age, nationality, previous schooling, and daily industrial environment. Yet no one of these factors can be ignored in successful night school work. School reports contain frequent references to the disastrous effects of attempting to train young boys or girls and adults in the same class. It is quite as difficult to meet in a group the needs of different nationalities. Some uniformity of grading on the basis of previous schooling would seem obviously desirable. The last factor, the daily industrial environment, is one not generally considered as demanding the teacher's attention, but it can not safely be ignored. In order to meet adequately individual needs in two hours in the evening, it would seem obvious that the true educator must know something of the industrial conditions surrounding his pupil ten hours during the day, and this would seem to be true whether the pupil is studying arithmetic or whether he is seeking skill in industry. The relation of the school to industry is convincingly illustrated when overtime in the factory keeps a girl away from school night after night until she leaves in discouragement.

From the point of view of the student the difficulties of attending night school after a hard day's work, an exhausting subway ride, and a hasty dinner are so great that unless the work is directly and thoughtfully adapted to his needs, the school will lose a pupil. This adaptation to individual needs must be secured in two ways: a careful grading of classes by consultation with each pupil at entrance, and as thorough a study as possible of each pupil by the teacher. In both directions the card record system is an important factor. Its use is not limited to a convenient basis for a statistical report, but it should primarily be designed to arouse the teacher's interest in her individual pupils and to provide her with definite information as a basis for class work.

Thus a system of records in evening school must meet several important requirements.

1. It should be the basis for consultation at entrance as to choice of subject.

2. It should inform the teacher at a glance, of the age, nationality, previous schooling, present occupation, hours of work, and regularity of attendance of each pupil.

3. It should provide the maximum amount of information with the minimum amount of clerical work on the part of the teacher.

4. It should adapt itself to frequent changes in the make-up of a class. For example, there are evening school classes with an average attendance of 20 and a total enrollment of 75 or more individuals who have attended one night or more in the course of the winter. An efficient system of records should make it possible to drop out the records of non-attendants, and at the same time be able to restore those who may return later in the year.

5. It should be a convenient basis for statistical reports.

6. It should be continuous, making it possible to watch the progress of pupils who may attend night school for several successive seasons.

7. It should provide data enabling teachers, principals and school authorities to watch results, to solve problems, and to plan changes. For example, we may name such important problems as the regularity of attendance compared in different classes, different neighborhoods, different nationalities, different ages, different occupations, and different months; the comparative efficiency of work in the first hour and the second hour of the evening session; need for industrial

training in evening schools and desirable occupations in which to experiment; the relation of evening schools to day schools; and the relation of factory laws to evening schools.

SYSTEM OF RECORDS SUGGESTED

In suggesting a system of record cards to meet these requirements, we have used the following guides:

1. The present system of record cards in the evening high schools, and the method of keeping roll books in evening elementary schools.
2. The uniform card record system now used in elementary day schools.
3. The cards planned last autumn by the Committee on Women's Work as a basis for the investigation already described.

The plan which we suggest, in brief, is to have two record cards, one to be kept on file in the principal's office, corresponding to the present admission book, and the other to be used by the teacher for records of attendance corresponding to the present roll books. The admission card would be filed alphabetically in the principal's office and would show the class to which each pupil had been assigned. The teacher's card might be perforated for use in a loose-leaf note book, thus combining the advantages of a roll book and a card record system. When a pupil had been discharged the teacher's card would be filed by classes in the principal's office, so that it could be at hand for reference by the principal at any time, and yet each teacher when preparing the annual statistical report could readily secure the records of all who had been in her class in the year. At the close of the year the teachers' cards could all be filed alphabetically in the admission file so that the complete record of each pupil could be found at the time of registration the following season. Obviously, the admission card and the teacher's card should be uniform in size.

2. Suggested Form of Admission Card

Last Name | First Name | Address | Course Applied For

Reg. No. Adm. Dis. Subjects 1st Hr. Room No. 2d Hr. Room No.

Transfers. Date From Room No. To Room No. Date From To

Date of Birth Age Country of Birth Years in U.S.

Name of Parent or Guardian Address Father's Birthplace

Occupation Employer's Name Address

Business of Firm for which you Work? What Work do you do for this Firm?

What time do you begin work in the morning? How many minutes do you have for lunch at noon? What time do you stop work in the evening? In what months do you work overtime?

Day Schools Attended – Elementary. (Name All.)

New York City–Public Parochial Private

U.S. outside New York (Name Places) Foreign (Name Places)

How old were you when you began School? Last Elementary School Attended Grade Reached

How old were you when you left? Did you Graduate? If under 16, state date of your Working Papers.

Day High Schools Attended Years Attended? Did you Graduate?

Other Schools Attended

Public Evening Schools Courses Taken

Business Schools Courses Taken

Other (Trade Schools, Art Schools, etc.)

Department of Education, The City of New York.
Evening School Form No. — '11

To be Filed in the Office of the Principal.

3. Suggested Form of Teacher's Record of Pupil

LAST NAME FIRST NAME | ADDRESS | ROOM NO. HR. / SUBJECT GRADE / SUBJECT OTHER HR. ROOM NO.

DATE ADMITTED DATE DISCHARGED REASON FOR DISCHARGE

DATE OF BIRTH COUNTRY OF BIRTH YRS. IN U.S. FATHER'S BIRTHPLACE

NAME OF PARENT OR GUARDIAN ADDRESS

OCCUPATION EMPLOYER'S NAME ADDRESS

BUSINESS OF FIRM AND PUPIL'S WORK

HOURS OF WORK: FROM A.M. TO P.M. MONTHS OF OVERTIME

DAY SCHOOLS ATTENDED – ELEMENTARY

NEW YORK CITY

PUBLIC PAROCHIAL PRIVATE GRADE REACHED

OUTSIDE NEW YORK, U.S. FOREIGN:

HIGH SCHOOLS

DAY HIGH SCHOOLS ATTENDED YEARS ATTENDED GRADUATION

OTHER SCHOOLS

PUBLIC EVENING SCHOOLS COURSES TAKEN

BUSINESS SCHOOLS TRADE SCHOOLS OTHER

DEPARTMENT OF EDUCATION, THE CITY OF NEW YORK
EVENING SCHOOL, FORM NO. — '11
TEACHER'S RECORD
TO BE RETURNED TO PRINCIPAL WHEN PUPIL IS TRANSFERED OR DISCHARGED

LAST NAME | FIRST NAME | ADDRESS | ROOM NO. | HR. | SUBJECT | TEACHER

SYMBOLS A = ADMITTED, D = DISCHARGED, a = ABSENT, / = PRESENT, T = TARDY, R = ABSENCE EXPLAINED

SCHOOL YEAR 191 to 191

RECORD OF ATTENDANCE

MONTH	1	2	3	4	5	6	7	8	9	10	11	12	13	14	15	16	17	18	19	20	21	22	23	24	25	26	27	28	29	30	31	TOTAL EVENINGS ABSENT	TOTAL EVENINGS PRESENT
SEPT.																																	
OCT.																																	
NOV.																																	
DEC.																																	
JAN.																																	
FEB.																																	
MAR.																																	
APRIL																																	
MAY																																	

STANDING			
SUBJ 1 %	SUBJ 3 %	PROMOTED TO	TOTAL HRS. ATTENDED
SUBJ 2 %	SUBJ. 4 %		% OF ATTENDANCE

The accompanying form, No. 2, is suggested for the admission card. Form 3 (3a the reverse side) is the teacher's record.

Comments

I. The Size of the Card. The size of the card should be determined in such a way as to secure uniformity, and convenient and adequate spacing of information. The size 3 by 5 now used in the evening high schools is not large enough for the details contemplated in the plan which we have suggested, nor can a 3 by 5 card be bound easily in a loose-leaf book, which seems a useful device for class room work while permitting afterward the permanent alphabetical filing of records. Nor does the 4 by 6 card used in day schools seem to be convenient for the sort of information needed to meet the needs of the changing and heterogeneous classes in evening schools. For these reasons we suggest the size of the accompanying cards, 5 by 8, as more convenient for the arrangement of data. (Size reduced in printing here.)

II. The Data Secured. A comparison of the data now secured in evening high schools with the data contained on these suggested record forms shows that no new subject has been introduced but that several subjects have been expanded to provide more details. In order of their appearance on the admission card No. 2 these are as follows:

1. Years in the United States.

   This fact supplements the information now required under the heading "Country of birth."

2. Birthplace of father.

   In a population like that in New York City, the national traits of pupils can not be taken into account as they should be unless the birthplace of the father be recorded. For example, the child of an Italian and the child of a Russian might both be recorded as native born, but the record would not be adequate in meeting their needs in evening school.

3. (a) What is the business of the firm for which you now work? (b) What work do you do for this firm?

These supplement the record of occupation. Numerous instances might be cited to show the need for both questions. For example, a girl may give her occupation as "sewing." Unless "the business of the firm" is known, it is an open question whether she is in the neckwear trade, the millinery trade, the dressmaking trade, or employed in making sheets and pillow cases. Yet the seasons, the demands on the worker, and other industrial conditions vary in these different industries.

If, on the other hand, merely the business of the firm be recorded with no explanation of the work done by the girl or boy, the teacher can not know what the pupil's real occupation may be. For example, the employes of a shirtwaist manufacturer may be telephone operators, stenographers, bookkeepers, machine operators, errand girls, and a maid in the dressing room.

Furthermore, details are necessary here to prevent vague, general grouping. For example, a comparison of our records, in which the girls answered these two questions, with the teacher's records in which the card provided space for "occupation" only showed that the term "factory worker" was used to cover such different processes as "human hair work," "trimming of babies' caps," "willowing on ostrich feathers," and "operating on shirtwaists." The teacher knew all these pupils only as "factory workers."

4. Questions regarding the hours of work and the months of overtime.

It is not likely that problems of evening schools, and, back of them, fundamental problems of the education of workers, will ever be solved until efforts are made to adjust schools to industries and industries to schools. Information secured by means of evening school records showing the hours of work in different occupations, and the season of overtime, would be one step in the direction of defining these problems of adjustment. Nor is such information remote from the immediate task of an evening school teacher. For example, here are the factors in a very common problem: a shirt-waist maker enrolled in an evening school in East 106th Street; home address, Third Avenue near 120th Street; business address, Bleecker Street; closing hour, 6 p.m.; months of overtime, January and February; probable result, irregular attendance in November and December when the cold weather begins and the short time between leaving the factory and beginning evening school seems shorter as the cold increases the fatigue of the journey. Then comes overtime in January and after losing so many evenings the girl is too discouraged to return to school in the spring. Knowledge of these facts in advance might have enabled the teacher through consultation with the pupil to give some individual help to counteract the discouragement of irregularity. When overtime work began, the labor department could have been notified, to prevent the lengthening of the working week beyond the legal limit. Especially ought such a procedure to be followed in the case of children under sixteen who can not legally be permitted to work in or in connection with a factory after 5 p.m. nor more than eight hours a day. Publication of information about the hours of work of women and children who attend evening schools would arouse public opinion, and tend gradually to shorten the hours of work and to strengthen the enforcement of labor laws. Until such action can be taken, the work of public evening schools will continue to be balked by the industrial conditions which their pupils encounter daily. Instead of such antagonism, the schools and the industries in an efficient community ought to cooperate in developing the intelligence and the strength of the workers. Unless the schools take steps to understand more thoroughly the industrial environment of their pupils, the day of such an ideal adjustment will be postponed indefinitely.

5. Questions regarding schools attended.

In the cards now used in evening high schools only four questions are asked regarding schooling: Last school attended? Year of leaving? Was this a day or an evening school? and, Did you graduate? It is not difficult to discover cases in which these questions would be blind alleys, not giving any clues to the child's school history. For example, suppose the last school were an evening school attended the preceding winter, or a business school attended five years ago. Results of the investigation made by the Committee on Women's Work show that English-speaking girls in evening schools this winter have attended a great variety of schools in a great variety of combinations. Schools of many foreign countries are represented. Schools in various sections of the United States, various types of schools, public, parochial, or private in New York City, and many business schools, trade or technical schools, and public evening schools appear on the cards of girls enrolled in the same class. To school authorities it is obvious without argument that an efficient evening school teacher will build on the previous school training of her pupils. But in ninety evenings, or one hundred and twenty evenings of the school term, she can not take the time to investigate her class unless it be part of her regular record work.

III. The Use of the Cards. The admission card has been designed to be filled by the pupil at entrance. Incidentally the filling of it would serve as a preliminary examination of the pupil's intelligence. The teacher's card is designed so that the information can readily be drawn from the admission card. Subjects and arrangement are almost identical, although more questions are asked on the admission card, while the teacher's card summarizes the important facts. The attendance record on the back of the teacher's card would seem less confusing than the present arrangement on the evening high school card, providing spaces to indicate groups of 10 evenings. It would seem also to provide a convenient basis for weekly and monthly reports, since the number of evenings attended each month can be totaled so easily.

So far as we have discovered, no system of evening school records has been worked out in any city with special reference to evening school needs and problems. The New York evening high schools have taken the lead. The department of education in New York may well be a pioneer now in planning a system to be used also in the evening elementary schools looking toward both economy of time in record keeping, and encouragement of a more thorough study of individual pupils.

Respectfully submitted,

THE COMMITTEE ON WOMEN'S WORK OF THE RUSSELL SAGE FOUNDATION.

May 27, 1911.

APPENDIX III

INVESTIGATION OF EVENING SCHOOL PUPILS IN PHILADELPHIA

IN the winter of 1912–13 the Public Education Association of Philadelphia made an investigation of pupils in evening schools of that city, distributing card records based in part upon the form used in the New York investigation described in this book. The Philadelphia study is not yet in print, nor have the results been fully interpreted, but certain salient facts may be noted. These have been secured from the manuscript of the report, courteously loaned us by the association. In Philadelphia 7,000 records were filled out, of which 6,410 were complete enough for tabulation. Of the number studied, 3,402 were in the elementary evening schools, 2,458 were evening high school students, and the remaining 550 were enrolled in the two evening trade schools.

Unlike the investigation in New York, the study in Philadelphia included both boys and girls, and the classes in English for foreigners were not omitted. Because of these differences in the scope of the inquiry and because the record cards are not identical, it is not wise to attempt detailed comparison of conditions in New York and Philadelphia. The important conclusions of the Philadelphia study may, however, be summarized as follows, stressing especially the facts secured regarding girls in the schools:

(1) Of the 6,410 investigated, about two-thirds, or 4,348, were boys, and one-third, or 2,062, were girls. In the evening high schools over 77 per cent, 1,906 of 2,458, were boys, showing apparently that the girls

were not taking advantage of the advanced courses. In the elementary schools the sexes were more equally represented, but of the 1,510 girls in these schools, 63 per cent, or 946, were foreigners, most of whom were enrolled in the courses in English. On the basis of these facts, the Philadelphia investigators conclude that, however adequately or inadequately Philadelphia is meeting the need of providing further training for her boys who must go to work at an early age, the aspect of the problem as it affects girls is still almost untouched.

(2) A study of the nationality of pupils showed that, as in New York, foreigners are eager to take advantage of evening school courses. About two-fifths, or 2,733 of 6,410 pupils in all the evening schools, were foreigners, and more than half of these foreign-born students, 1,594, were Russians. A comparison of nativity in evening schools with the nativity of the Philadelphia population showed a far larger percentage of Russians in the schools than their importance in the population would justify; while it was found that Germans, English, and Irish do not attend the schools in numbers proportionate to their representation in the population.

(3) Young people predominate in the classes in the Philadelphia evening schools; 68 per cent, or 4,335 of the 6,337 reporting their ages, were under twenty years of age; 1,138, or 18 per cent, were under sixteen. In the year of the investigation, 13,740 children between fourteen and sixteen secured work certificates in Philadelphia; yet only 8.3 per cent (1,138) of these children were found in the evening schools so far as the records of the investigation showed. On the basis of these facts the investigators conclude that the evening schools do not in any sense serve as continuation schools for the fourteen- to sixteen-year-old worker; that it is doubtful whether any attempt should be made to secure the attendance of these children during night hours after a day's work; and that there is a crying need for some form of education established by law which

shall furnish the necessary continuation training for this group. It is very significant that of the 1,138 under sixteen, 113, or 10 per cent, were not employed, although they had left day school under the provisions of the law permitting fourteen- and fifteen-year-old children to go to work. It was never the intent of this law to let these children drop out of school and substitute night courses for day courses, or remain out of school altogether, if they were not employed by day.

(4) Only 14 per cent, or 876 of 6,190 reporting on this point, had ever received any day schooling after their sixteenth birthday, while 65 per cent, or 4,052, had left school at the age of fourteen or earlier, and 4 per cent, or 227, had never attended any school. These figures included the foreign born, whose opportunities in their home countries had been very limited.

(5) As in New York, distinct differences with reference to schooling were discovered in the different occupational groups. Pupils in domestic service and the small group in agriculture, as a rule, left school at the earliest age, with manufacturing next, while those employed in trade and transportation and in professional pursuits had a longer period of schooling.

(6) Unlike the study in New York, the Philadelphia investigation included information about wages. The question asked was: "How much do you make a week?" The result showed that of the total number of 5,510 reporting on this question, 3,000, or 54 per cent, were receiving less than $8.00 a week.

Of the 1,632 girls and women in the group, reporting wages, 1,085, or 66 per cent, were receiving less than $8.00, while of the 3,878 men and boys, 1,915, or 49 per cent, were in the group earning less than $8.00. Only 84, or 1.5 per cent, of the entire group were earning $20 or more, and these were all men. Only 10 girls reported a wage of $16 or over, and none of these received as much as $20.

(7) Among the Philadelphia evening school pupils a great variety of occupations are represented, including, of course, the trades most important in Philadelphia

—the textile industry, metal work, the dressmaking and clothing trades, weaving of cloth, the making and trimming of hats, and the manufacture of hosiery and knit goods. For the most part, however, these evening school pupils are not receiving any instruction in the evening which is related to their daily work, and only 31 per cent are taking any of the vocational courses offered. The investigators conclude that the evening school courses are not adapted to the needs of the workers; that they should be reorganized along the lines of the industries which have the largest development in Philadelphia; that they should offer courses of more definite practical use in these industries; and that they should be made to serve the purposes of vocational schools for the older workers.

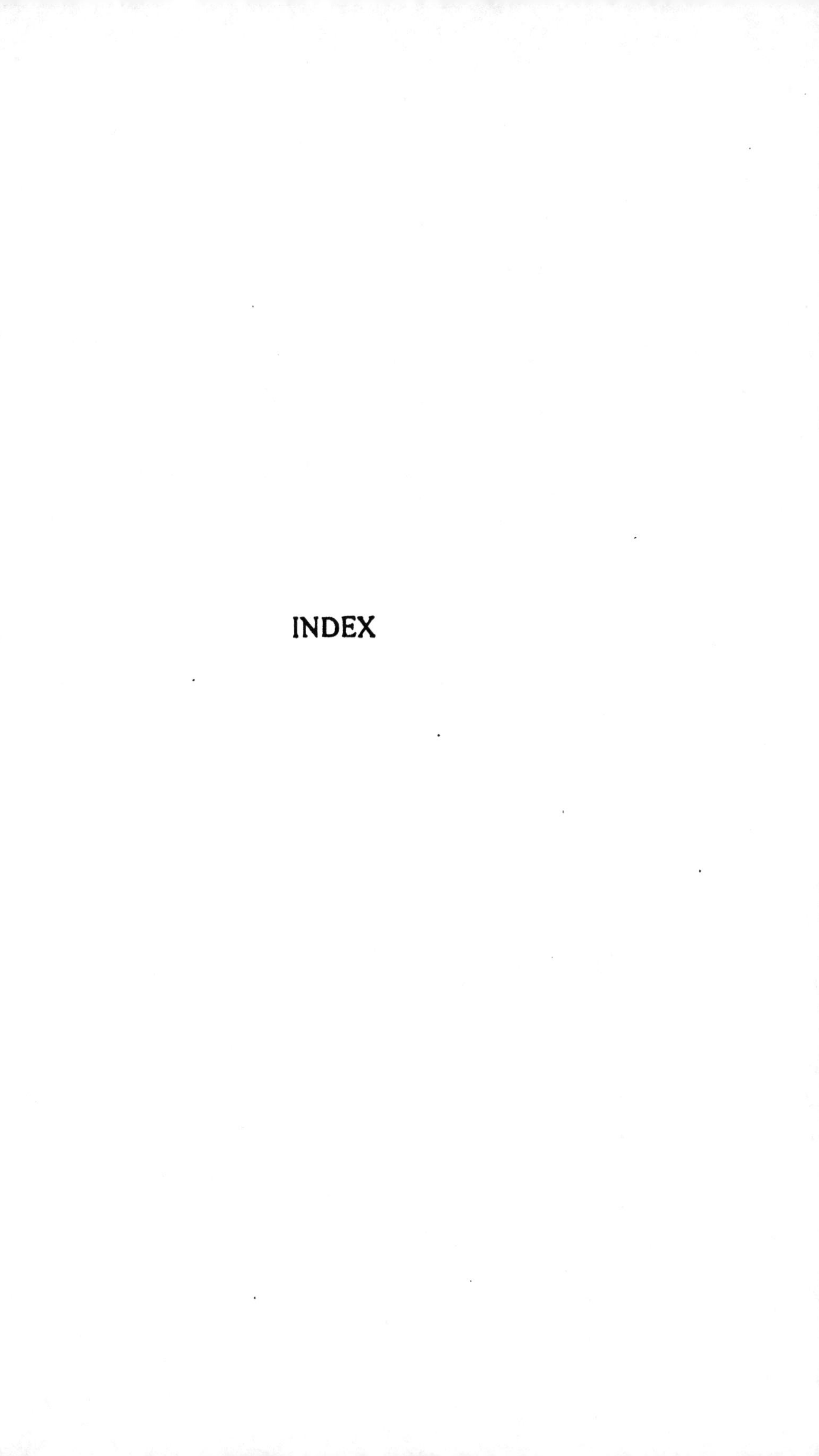

INDEX

INDEX

INDEX

INDEX